THE MORMON FAITH

A New Look at Christianity

Robert L. Millet

SHADOW MOUNTAIN

Library of Congress Cataloging-in-Publication Data

Millet, Robert L.
    The Mormon faith : a new look at Christianity /
Robert L. Millet.
       p.   cm.
    Includes bibliographical references and index.
    ISBN 1-57345-359-5
    1. Church of Jesus Christ of Latter-day Saints—Doctrines.
2. Mormon Church—Doctrines. I. Title.
BX8635.2.M545   1998
289.3'32—dc21   97-48600
                                                            CIP

Printed in the United States of America   72082-6351

10 9 8 7 6 5 4 3 2 1

THE MORMON FAITH

CONTENTS

CONTENTS

PREFACE

Many in the religious world have taken the time to learn about The Church of Jesus Christ of Latter-day Saints. Sadly, the polarization of people by available literature on Joseph Smith and the Latter-day Saint faith—whether antagonistic or apologetic—has prevented many who have sincere interest from receiving a balanced presentation. One need not become either a convert to or a crusader for the LDS Church to understand the phenomenon or the people. This book is written not to convert but to aid in understanding. And if anything is needed in this complex and confusing world, it is understanding.

There is certainly benefit to be had in studying a religious experience or a theological perspective from outside the faith; the scholarly detachment may allow for some degree of objectivity. But some things can be fully understood only from within the fold. I have spent the past twenty-five years studying the Church's history and theology. My major area of study in my doctoral training at Florida State University allowed me to look beyond the bounds of the LDS faith and attempt to assess Joseph Smith's place and impact upon the larger spectrum of religion and religious life in America. And so I have what I feel is the needed background to write an objective study; I am, however, a member of the Church, and I have chosen to write as an insider.

This work draws heavily upon the teachings of Joseph Smith, the first prophet and president of the Church, as well as the Bible and other LDS scriptures. In addition, I have quoted numerous other Church leaders from both the nineteenth and twentieth centuries to establish the Church's view on this or that matter. I hasten to add that this book is at best an introduction to the faith and that all questions cannot be answered on every issue. That is one of the drawbacks of an introduction. In order to get at this problem, however, chapter 14 is devoted to some of the most frequently asked questions, as well as a few of the more sensitive issues in the Church.

The continuing growth and appeal of the LDS Church cannot be explained wholly by pointing to "the good life" practiced by the members of the Church. Doctrine is a significant part of the religion of the Latter-day Saints, and very often theology is what strikes a consonant cord in the minds and hearts of interested people. Further, the Latter-day Saints believe strongly that their style of life grows out of their theology; we cannot really understand why they do what they do or why they are what they are until we understand what they believe. This book will therefore emphasize what most people know *least* about the Latter-day Saints—their doctrine and their theology. Millions have heard about their health code, about polygamy, about Brigham Young and the exodus across the plains, about their generally conservative political posture, about their welfare program, and even about their athletes and entertainers. But few know about

- the LDS concept of God;
- their teachings about Jesus Christ;
- the LDS view of the canon of scripture;
- Joseph Smith's translation of the Bible;
- the premortal nature of men and women;
- their view of grace and works;
- what really goes on in LDS temples; and,
- their view of life after death.

These are but a few of the many doctrinal matters treated in this book. Emphasis will be on fundamental doctrines and practices of the faith.

I am not authorized to speak for The Church of Jesus Christ of Latter-day Saints. What I write, therefore, is my own view of things and thus not an official publication or pronouncement of either the Church or of Brigham Young University, where I serve on the Religion faculty—for many years as Dean of Religious Education and Professor of Ancient Scripture. I am also fully aware that some Mormons who read what follows—Latter-day Saints all along the spectrum of what might be called orthodox belief and practice—might differ with my interpretation of the facts or explanation of some doctrines or practices. That is to be expected. But again, I have chosen to represent as best I can the faith of The Church of Jesus Christ of Latter-day Saints, with headquarters in Salt Lake City, Utah. I feel confident that what is written represents a majority view.

At the time of the Church's formal organization on April 6, 1830, in Fayette, New York, there were six official members. Projections by sociologists of religion suggest that at present rates of growth, the LDS population worldwide in the year 2080 could be somewhere between 60 million and 265 million. Whether one chooses to pursue his or her study of the LDS faith out of sheer curiosity or more academically from a sociological, historical, anthropological, or theological point of view, there is a great deal to investigate. The movement that began as a frontier faith will undoubtedly continue in a healthy and unhindered fashion to influence the religious world.

ACKNOWLEDGMENTS

In the preparation of this work I am indebted to many persons. I express special appreciation to Sheri L. Dew and Ronald A. Millett for their interest and encouragement in the project. For Jack Lyon's patient and perceptive editorial assistance I am also grateful. Lori Soza has, as always, been efficient and painstaking in moving the manuscript through its various stages prior to publication.

FOUNDATIONAL

EVENTS

M embers of The Church of Jesus Christ of Latter-day Saints (referred to hereafter as Latter-day Saints, LDS, or Mormon) believe in God. They believe that Jesus of Nazareth is the Son of God and the Savior of humankind. They believe in observing high moral standards and in honoring and sustaining the laws of the land. They believe there is purpose in life, and that happiness is the object of our existence and the product of a well-lived life. Many of these matters of faith and practice, matters the Latter-day Saints share with men and women of goodwill throughout the earth, will be treated in more detail in subsequent chapters. For now we will start at the beginning.

THE SETTING

One simply cannot understand the Latter-day Saints without at least some understanding of their origins. The Church as we know it came into being in the early nineteenth century. The population of our young nation doubled in the first quarter of that century. It was a time of revolution, what some historians have called the "Second American

Revolution," a time of upheaval, of movement—social, political, economic, and religious. There was a movement in values and ideology as well as topography. Alexis de Tocqueville characterized the age as follows: "In the United States a man builds a house in which to spend his old age, and he sells it before the roof is on; he plants a garden, and leaves it just as the trees are coming into bearing."[1] Orestes Brownson, a prominent thinker of the time, explained, "No tolerable observer of the signs of the time can have failed to perceive that we are, in this vicinity at least, in the midst of a very important revolution; a revolution which extends to every department of thought, and threatens to change ultimately the whole moral aspect of society. Everything is loosened from its old fastenings, and is floating no one can tell whither."[2]

This was the age of Restorationism, an era in America's history when men and women read the Bible, believed its story and message, and sought for a return to "the ancient order of things." Many longed for the reestablishment of primitive Christianity; others desired once more to enjoy the spiritual gifts and outpourings that had once graced the ancients. A classic illustration of one imbued with such desires was Alexander Campbell. Thomas and Alexander Campbell came to America from Ireland. Educated and trained as Presbyterian ministers in Scotland, Thomas Campbell and his son began another of the many campaigns against creeds and a strict Calvinism. Thomas had arrived in America first and, after having obtained a pastorate in a Presbyterian church in southwestern Pennsylvania, had managed to incur the wrath of the synod for teaching what were perceived as heretical doctrines. Campbell rejected the notion that the church should hold the Westminster Confession of Faith as a term of communion. He denied that faith came through some mystical-emotional experience, stressing that faith resulted rather from "an intelligent response to the mind of evi-

---

[1] *Democracy in America*, 2 vols. (New York: Alfred A. Knopf, 1945), 2:164.

[2] *Boston Quarterly Review*, 3 vols. (Boston: Cambridge Press, 1840), 3:265.

dence."[3] After dismissal by the Presbyterians, Thomas continued to teach his doctrines to the farmers in western Pennsylvania and organized the "Christian Association of Washington" in 1809. This society stressed "a pure Gospel ministry, that shall reduce to practice that whole form of doctrine, worship, discipline, and government, expressly revealed and enjoined in the word of God."[4]

Alexander Campbell joined his father in America in 1809, learned of the beliefs and practices of the movement, and assumed leadership. He accepted the doctrine of believer's baptism by immersion, was baptized, and in 1811 accepted the pastorate at the Brush Run Baptist Church in what is now Bethany, West Virginia. Campbell's adherence to his Restorationist beliefs proved a serious concern to the Baptists, and he was rejected by many Baptist colleagues in the ministry. In 1823 the younger Campbell began editing a magazine entitled the *Christian Baptist,* the title of which was eventually changed to the *Millennial Harbinger,* the latter title evidencing a belief in the imminence of Christ's second coming. Campbell's dissatisfaction with nominal Christianity is apparent in a statement from the first volume of the *Christian Baptist:* "We are convinced, fully convinced, that the whole head is sick, and the whole heart faint of modern fashionable Christianity."[5] In addition, Campbell the iconoclast "condemned all beliefs and practices that could not be validated by apostolic mandates. He proclaimed that missionary societies, tract societies, Bible societies, synods, associations, and theological seminaries were inconsistent with pure religion."[6]

Alexander Campbell's disillusionment with nineteenth-century religion was not an isolated perception. As late as 1838 Ralph Waldo Emerson stated in his famous "Divinity

---

[3] See W. E. Garrison and A. T. DeGroot, *The Disciples of Christ* (St. Louis: Mo., Bethany Press, 1958), pp. 133–39.

[4] Ibid., pp. 146–48.

[5] *Christian Baptist,* 7 vols., 13th ed., rev. Edited by D. S. Burnet (Bethany, West Virginia: H. S. Bosworth, 1861), 1:33.

[6] Milton V. Backman, Jr., *American Religions and the Rise of Mormonism* (Salt Lake City: Deseret Book Co., 1970), p. 241.

School Address" at Harvard that "the need was never greater of new revelation than now." Further, "the Church seems to totter to its fall, almost all life extinct." Continuing, "I look forward for the hour when the supreme Beauty, which ravished the souls of those Eastern men, and chiefly of those Hebrews, and through their lips spoke oracles to all time, shall speak in the west also."[7]

A number of later LDS Church leaders spoke of their own quest for truth and of the frustrations they felt before their encounter with Joseph Smith. Brigham Young stated, "My mind was opened to conviction, and I knew that the Christian world had not the religion that Jesus and the Apostles taught. I knew that there was not a Bible Christian on earth within my knowledge."[8] Wilford Woodruff, fourth president of the Church, said, "I did not join any church, believing that the Church of Christ in its true organization did not exist upon the earth."[9] Willard Richards, later a counselor to Brigham Young, became "convinced that the sects were all wrong, and that God had no church on earth, but that he would soon have a church on earth whose creed would be the truth."[10]

JOSEPH SMITH'S FIRST VISION

Nothing of consequence emerges in a social or intellectual vacuum, and Joseph Smith and the work set in motion were no different. What began as a frontier faith through the work of an obscure farm boy and would later survive and blossom into a worldwide religious movement did not come into being in "dry ground." Indeed, the ground was prepared through a general dissatisfaction of large groups of people with mainline religious bodies. The roots of the new religion would sink

---

[7] Delivered before the senior class at the Harvard Divinity School, Cambridge, Massachusetts, July 15, 1838; in *Theology in America,* ed. Sydney E. Ahlstrom (Indianapolis: Bobbs-Merrill, 1967), pp. 306, 315–16.
[8] *Journal of Discourses,* 26 vols. (Liverpool: F. D. Richards and Sons, 1851–86), 5:75.
[9] Ibid., 4:99.
[10] *History of The Church of Jesus Christ of Latter-day Saints,* 7 vols., edited by B. H. Roberts (Salt Lake City: Deseret Book Co., 1957), 2:470.

deep into the soil because individuals were anxious for a "new revelation."

Into this world of nineteenth-century foment came Joseph Smith, Jr. He was born in Sharon, Vermont, on December 23, 1805, the fourth of nine children of Joseph and Lucy Mack Smith. His family moved thereafter to Tunbridge, Vermont; Lebanon, New Hampshire; and Norwich, Vermont. Finally in 1814 they settled in Western New York. After two years of hard labor and financial strain, Joseph Smith, Sr., purchased 100 acres of unimproved land two miles south of Palmyra, New York, on the Palmyra-Manchester town line. In commenting on the religious activity in his own area, young Joseph mentioned that some time in the second year after the family's move to Manchester, "there was in the place where we lived an unusual excitement on the subject of religion." He continued his report by explaining that the excitement "commenced with the Methodists, but soon became general among all the sects in that region of country. Indeed, the whole district of country seemed affected by it, and great multitudes united themselves to the different religious parties." (Pearl of Great Price, Joseph Smith—History 1:5.) Between 1816 and 1821 revivals were reported in more towns and more settlers joined churches than at any previous time in New York's history.[11] During this period of religious explosion, the Smith family was proselyted by the Presbyterian sect. Young Joseph (in his fifteenth year) leaned toward the Methodists and felt some desire to join them. Four members of the family became officially associated with the Presbyterians, but Joseph remained an interested investigator of truth without fully committing himself to any church.

Joseph attended many of the revivals with family members and became concerned for the salvation of his own soul. In addition, he was particularly troubled about which of all the religious denominations was correct and which he should

---

[11] See Milton V. Backman, Jr., "Awakenings in the Burned-Over District: New Light on the Historical Setting of the First Vision," *Brigham Young University Studies*, vol. 9, no. 3, spring 1969, p. 302.

join. Tradition has it that at one of the revivals a minister quoted from James 1:5–6 in the New Testament ("If any of you lack wisdom, let him ask of God") and encouraged the congregation to undertake their religious quest through prayer as well as study. The fourteen-year-old then returned to his home and read the same passage from the family Bible. He later wrote of this experience, "Never did any passage of scripture come with more power to the heart of man than this did at this time to mine. It seemed to enter with great force into every feeling of my heart. I reflected on it again and again, knowing that if any person needed wisdom from God, I did; for how to act I did not know." (Pearl of Great Price, Joseph Smith—History 1:12.)

Joseph reported that soon thereafter he walked to a grove of trees not far from his father's farm and knelt to pray. He later wrote, "Information was what I most desired at this time, and with a fixed determination to obtain it I called upon the Lord for the first time."[12] It was the spring of 1820. In writing of that occasion almost twenty years later, Joseph Smith made the following remarkable claim:

> After I had retired to the place where I had previously designed to go, having looked around me, and finding myself alone, I kneeled down and began to offer up the desire of my heart to God. I had scarcely done so, when immediately I was seized upon by some power which entirely overcame me, and had such an astonishing influence over me as to bind my tongue so that I could not speak. Thick darkness gathered around me, and it seemed to me for a time as if I were doomed to sudden destruction.
>
> But, exerting all my powers to call upon God to deliver me out of the power of this enemy which had seized upon me, and at the very moment when I was ready to sink into despair and abandon myself to destruction—not to an imaginary ruin, but to the power of some actual being from the unseen world, who had such marvelous power as I had

---

[12] 1835 account of the First Vision, in Milton V. Backman, Jr., *Joseph Smith's First Vision*, 2nd ed. (Salt Lake City: Bookcraft, 1980), p. 159.

never before felt in any being—just at this moment of great alarm, I saw a pillar of light exactly over my head, above the brightness of the sun, which descended gradually until it fell upon me.

It no sooner appeared than I found myself delivered from the enemy which held me bound. When the light rested upon me I saw two Personages, whose brightness and glory defy all description, standing above me in the air. One of them spake unto me, calling me by name and said, pointing to the other—This is my Beloved Son. Hear Him! (Pearl of Great Price, Joseph Smith—History 1:15–17.)

In an earlier account of the same phenomenon, Joseph explained that "a pillar of light above the brightness of the sun at noon day came down from above and rested upon me and I was filled with the spirit of God. The Lord opened the heavens upon me and I saw the Lord and he spake unto me, saying, Joseph, my son, thy sins are forgiven thee. Go thy way. Walk in my statutes and keep my commandments."[13] In 1842 Joseph Smith prepared a brief history of the Mormons. The history contains the following description of the theophany:

While fervently engaged in supplication my mind was taken away from the objects with which I was surrounded, and I was enwrapped in a heavenly vision and saw two glorious personages who exactly resembled each other in features and likeness, surrounded with a brilliant light which eclipsed the sun at noon day. They told me that all religious denominations were believing in incorrect doctrines, and that none of them was acknowledged of God as his church and kingdom. And I was expressly commanded to "go not after them," at the same time receiving a promise that the fulness of the gospel should at some time be made known unto me.[14]

---

[13] 1832 account, in ibid., p. 157; punctuation corrected.
[14] 1842 account, in ibid., p. 169.

This experience has come to be known by Latter-day Saints as "Joseph Smith's First Vision" and is central to their faith. They believe in God, in Jesus Christ, and in the Holy Bible. They also believe in modern and continuing revelation and modern prophets, and the First Vision is foundational to such beliefs.

The unfolding of Joseph Smith's doctrinal beliefs and the early development of the faith would entail a lengthy process over the next twenty-four years of his life. At the same time, the prophet-leader and his followers came to extract definite theological principles from the First Vision, such as (1) a belief in a literal Satanic being bent upon the overthrow of all that is good; (2) the reality of God the Father as a separate and distinct personage from the resurrected Jesus Christ; (3) the concept that a universal apostasy or falling away had taken place in the first-century Christian Church, and that no religious denomination on earth had authority to act in the name of God; (4) the need for a restoration—more than a reformation—in order that saving truths and powers might be given anew to mortals on earth; and (5) the confidence that it was possible for men and women to pray in faith, to commune with their Maker, and to know the things of God. Joseph Smith would later state his position in regard to the reality of his experience: "Though I was hated and persecuted for saying that I had seen a vision, yet it was true; . . . I knew it, and I knew that God knew it, and I could not deny it, neither dared I do it; at least I knew that by so doing I would offend God, and come under condemnation." (Pearl of Great Price, Joseph Smith—History 1:25.)

After the experience, Joseph wrote, "My soul was filled with love, and for many days I could rejoice with great joy. The Lord was with me but I could find none that would believe the heavenly vision."[15] In speaking more specifically of the opposition he faced, he wrote of an encounter with a Methodist minister some days after the vision: "I took occasion to give him an account of the vision which I had had. I

---

[15] 1832 account, in ibid., p. 157; punctuation corrected.

8

was greatly surprised at his behavior; he treated my communication not only lightly, but with great contempt, saying it was all of the devil, that there were no such things as visions or revelations in these days; that all such things had ceased with the apostles, and that there would never be any more of them." (Pearl of Great Price, Joseph Smith—History 1:21.)

THE GROWTH OF THE CHURCH

Some three years after his first vision, Joseph claimed to have been visited by an angel named Moroni, an ancient American prophet who returned to deliver a scriptural record that came to be known as the Book of Mormon. We will discuss the Book of Mormon as a part of the expanded canon of LDS scripture in the next chapter.

Early on, Joseph Smith taught that a vision or revelation from God was not sufficient to represent Deity. He sensed, like Roger Williams, the founder of the Baptist Church, that the authority to act in the name of God was not to be found on earth, that priesthood had been lost with the death of the original apostles. John Winthrop, one of Williams's contemporaries, noted that Williams had concluded that the Protestants were "not . . . able to derive the authority . . . from the apostles" but "conceived God would raise up some apostolic power."[16] After a while Roger Williams renounced the views of the Baptists and "turned seeker, i.e., to wait for new apostles to restore Christianity. He believed the Christian religion to have been . . . corrupted and disfigured in what he called the 'apostasy,' . . . and that there was need of a special commission, to restore the modes of positive worship, according to the original institution."[17]

It was while translating the Book of Mormon that Joseph Smith and his scribe continued to encounter references to

---

[16] John Winthrop, *History of New England*, 2 vols., edited by James Kendall Hosmer (New York: Barnes and Noble, 1946), 1:309.
[17] John Callender, *An Historical Discourse, on the Civil and Religious Affairs of the Colony of Rhode Island and Province Plantations* (Boston, 1739; reprinted in *Collections of the Rhode Island Historical Society*, Providence, 1838), 4:109–11.

baptism and other ordinances (sacraments), as well as the need for proper authority to perform the same. Feeling the need to inquire of God on the matter, they knelt in prayer on May 15, 1829, on the banks of the Susquehanna River near Harmony, Pennsylvania. According to Joseph, an angel who called himself John, known in the New Testament as John the Baptist (the one who had prepared the way for and baptized Jesus), appeared, laid his hands upon their heads, and ordained them to what Joseph Smith called the Aaronic Priesthood. The Aaronic Priesthood, known also as the Lesser Priesthood or the Preparatory Priesthood, contained the power to teach and preach, to call to repentance, to baptize, and to ordain others to the same authority. John explained that "he acted under the direction of Peter, James and John, who held the keys of the Priesthood of Melchizedek, which Priesthood, he said, would in due time be conferred on us." (Pearl of Great Price, Joseph Smith—History 1:72.) Joseph Smith stated that within weeks the three ancient apostles did in fact appear and bestow the higher or Melchizedek Priesthood. This authority contained the power to confirm individuals members of the Church after water baptism and confer the gift of the Holy Ghost. In addition, Joseph taught that the power he received from Peter, James, and John included the holy apostleship, the same authority given by Jesus anciently to bind and seal on earth and in heaven. (See Matthew 16:16–19; 18:18.) We will speak more of the organization of the Church, general and local ecclesiastical structure, and the rights and powers of the priesthood in chapter 8.

On April 6, 1830, Joseph Smith met with a large group at Fayette, New York, to formally organize what was called on that day the Church of Christ. Later the name was changed to the Church of the Latter Day Saints, and in 1838 to The Church of Jesus Christ of Latter-day Saints. Joseph Smith was then and thereafter acknowledged and sustained by his followers as a prophet, seer, revelator, and apostle, and as first elder of the Church. Missionaries were sent out from the earliest days, and congregations of Saints (followers of Christ and baptized members of the Church) were established in New

York and Pennsylvania. By 1831 there were two church centers, one in Kirtland, Ohio, and one in Independence, Missouri. Severe persecution in Independence in 1833 and troubles in Ohio in the late 1830s forced the people into other parts of Missouri, and eventually the Mormons left the state in 1838 and settled on the banks of the Mississippi River at Commerce, Illinois. There, from 1839 to 1846, they enjoyed a brief season of peace and prosperity and built a city that came to be known as Nauvoo, the "city beautiful." Nauvoo grew during the time the Saints were there to become the second largest city in Illinois.

Missionaries were sent abroad, and tens of thousands, especially from Great Britain, converted to the Church. Many of these left their homelands as part of a modern gathering and came to America, the home of their newfound faith. But persecution and contention seemed to be ever a part of the lives of Joseph Smith and his followers. Fearing the Mormon prophet's increasing social and political strength and the capacity of the growing Church to wield more and more influence in the state—and being distressed by a number of the beliefs and practices of the Latter-day Saints, including plural marriage—the enemies of the Church (some from among dissident and disaffected members) eventually murdered Joseph Smith and his brother Hyrum in Carthage, Illinois, on June 27, 1844.

Many across the nation felt that The Church of Jesus Christ of Latter-day Saints would, with the death of its charismatic leader, succumb to this final, stunning blow. But the Saints proved that their faith was not founded in a mortal man; by now the personal conviction of the truthfulness of what Joseph Smith had established was deep, while the vision was broad. There was left to Brigham Young the responsibility to regroup the Saints and prepare them for departure from Illinois and then an arduous and now-famous trek across the plains to the Great Basin and what is now Salt Lake City, Utah. The formal date of entry into the Salt Lake Valley was July 24, 1847. Brigham Young served as the Church's second president for thirty years, and during that

time, although the Mormons enjoyed some degree of auton-
omy in their remote gathering place, there were ongoing
struggles with the U.S. government over plural marriage and
what was perceived to be the growing theocratic power of
Brigham Young himself. Those struggles continued through
the nineteenth century until plural marriage was formally
discontinued in 1890 and Utah became the forty-fifth state in
the union in 1896. Growth and expansion throughout the
world have characterized the twentieth-century church, and
the movement set in motion by Joseph Smith continues to
wield an influence.

CHAPTER 2

SCRIPTURE AND THE EXPANDING CANON

I remember very well sitting in a doctoral course entitled "Seminar on Biblical Studies" in the late 1970s. There were eight of us in the course, as I recall, from various religious backgrounds—two Southern Baptists, a couple of Methodists, a Reform Jew, a Roman Catholic, a Nazarene, and a Latter-day Saint. It was an excellent class and helped introduce me to the vocabulary of the academic study of religion, as well as some of the problems and challenges of biblical scholarship. The professor, a former Methodist minister, was a superb instructor. He was organized, well prepared, and considerate of students. He responded well to questions and was always available for consultation. We studied various topics, including the nature of scripture, covenant, prophecy, interpretation, authorship, and the dating of scriptural records. One of the things that stands out in my mind is our discussion of the canon of scripture. We had covered in some detail the historical roots of the Old and New Testament canons and had discussed at some length the relationship between canonicity and authority of scripture; that is, we had debated whether a document belonged in the canon because it was considered authoritative, or whether it was considered authoritative because it was included in the canon.

For two periods the instructor had emphasized that the word *canon*—referring, of course, to the biblical books that are generally included in the Judeo-Christian collection—implied the rule of faith, the standard against which we measure what is acceptable. Further, he stated that the canon, if the word meant anything at all, was *closed, fixed, set,* and *established.* I look back at my notes more than two decades later and realize that he must have stressed those four words at least ten times. I noticed in the second period that the instructor seemed a bit uneasy. I remember thinking that something must be wrong. Without warning, he stopped what he was doing, banged his fist on the table, turned to me, and said, "Mr. Millet, will you please explain to this group the Latter-day Saint concept of canon, especially given your acceptance of the Book of Mormon and other books of scripture beyond the Bible?" I was startled. Stumped. Certainly surprised. I paused for several seconds, looked up at the board, saw the now very familiar four words written under the word *canon,* and said somewhat shyly, "Well, I suppose you could say that the Latter-day Saints believe the canon of scripture is *open, flexible,* and *expanding!*" We spent much of the rest of the period trying to make sense out of what I had just said.

THE LATTER-DAY SAINTS AND THE BIBLE

Joseph Smith loved the Bible. It was his pondering upon a biblical passage that started his quest to know the will of the Almighty. Most of his sermons, writings, and letters are laced with quotations or paraphrasing summaries of biblical passages and precepts, from both the Old and New Testaments. Joseph once remarked that one can "see God's handwriting in the sacred volume; and he who reads it oftenest will like it best."[1] He believed that the Bible represented God's word to

---

[1] *Teachings of the Prophet Joseph Smith,* selected by Joseph Fielding Smith (Salt Lake City: Deseret Book Co., 1976), p. 56; cited hereafter as *Teachings.*

humanity, and he gloried in the truths and timeless lessons it contained.

The Completeness of the Bible. From his earliest days, however, Joseph did not believe that the Bible was complete, nor did he feel that religious difficulties could necessarily be handled quickly by turning to the Old or New Testaments for help. After speaking of how James 1:5–6 had made such a deep impression upon his soul, he wrote, "I reflected on it again and again, knowing that if any person needed wisdom from God, I did; . . . for the teachers of religion of the different sects understood the same passages of scripture so differently as to destroy all confidence in settling the question by an appeal to the Bible." (Pearl of Great Price, Joseph Smith— History 1:12.) On another occasion he spoke concerning his belief in ongoing revelation from God:

> From what we can draw from the Scriptures relative to the teaching of heaven, we are induced to think that much instruction has been given to man since the beginning which we do not possess now. This may not agree with the opinions of some of our friends who are bold to say that we have everything written in the Bible which God ever spoke to man since the world began, and that if He had ever said anything more we should certainly have received it. . . . We have what we have, and the Bible contains what it does contain: but to say that God never said anything more to man than is there recorded, would be saying at once that we have at last received a revelation: for it must require one to advance thus far, because it is nowhere said in that volume by the mouth of God that He would not, after giving what is there contained, speak again; and if any man has found out for a fact that the Bible contains all that God ever revealed to man he has ascertained it by an immediate revelation.[2]

In a letter to his uncle, Silas Smith, Joseph wrote in the same vein in 1833 of the need for continual direction through prophets:

---

[2] Ibid., p. 61.

Seeing that the Lord has never given the world to understand by anything heretofore revealed that he had ceased forever to speak to his creatures when sought unto in a proper manner, why should it be thought a thing incredible that he should be pleased to speak again in these last days for their salvation? Perhaps you may be surprised at this assertion that I should say "for the salvation of his creatures in these last days" since we have already in our possession a vast volume of his word [the Bible] which he has previously given. But you will admit that the word spoken to Noah was not sufficient for Abraham. . . . Isaac, the promised seed, was not required to rest his hope upon the promises made to his father Abraham, but was privileged with the assurance of his [God's] approbation in the sight of heaven by the direct voice of the Lord to him. . . .

I have no doubt but that the holy prophets and apostles and saints in the ancient days were saved in the kingdom of God. . . . I may believe that Enoch walked with God. I may believe that Abraham communed with God and conversed with angels. . . . I may believe that Elijah was taken to heaven in a chariot of fire with fiery horses. I may believe that the saints saw the Lord and conversed with him face to face after his resurrection. I may believe that the Hebrew Church came to Mount Zion and unto the city of the living God, the heavenly Jerusalem, and to an innumerable company of angels. I may believe that they looked into eternity and saw the Judge of all, and Jesus the Mediator of the new covenant; but will all this purchase an assurance for me, or waft me to the regions of eternal day with my garments spotless, pure, and white? Or, must I not rather obtain for myself, by my own faith and diligence, in keeping the commandments of the Lord, an assurance of salvation for myself? And have I not an equal privilege with the ancient saints? And will not the Lord hear my prayers, and listen to my cries as soon [as] he ever did to theirs, if I come to him in the manner they did? Or is he a respecter of persons?[3]

---

[3] *The Personal Writings of Joseph Smith*, edited by Dean C. Jessee (Salt Lake City: Deseret Book Co., 1984), pp. 297–301; spelling and punctuation corrected.

The Inerrancy of the Bible. One of the LDS articles of faith states, "We believe the Bible to be the word of God as far as it is translated correctly." (Pearl of Great Price, Articles of Faith 1:8.) It appears that Joseph Smith meant to convey what is generally associated with the term *transmitted;* there was certainly more involved in how we got the Bible than translation matters, including copying, adding to, taking from, and interpretation, as well as problems of translation from the ancient tongues. In 1843 he added, "I believe the Bible as it read when it came from the pen of the original writers. Ignorant translators, careless transcribers, or designing and corrupt priests have committed many errors."[4] He felt that many plain and precious truths had been taken from the Bible before the documents were compiled into what we now know as the Old and New Testaments. This was one of the reasons Joseph Smith felt called to initiate a *restoration* of truth and power, not simply a reformation of existing religious matters. Latter-day Saints are obviously not Catholic, but they are not Protestant, either; they did not break away from the Mother Church, nor did they seek to reform her. They thus speak of the fullness of the gospel of Jesus Christ being restored through Joseph Smith, not the least of which was doctrinal and theological matters once clearly taught or practiced but since lost to the world through the centuries.

Thus Joseph Smith did not hold a traditional belief in the infallibility or inerrancy of the Bible. He believed, to be sure, that the essential message of the Bible was true and from God. We could say that he believed it was "God's word." I am not so certain that he or modern Church leaders would be convinced that every sentence recorded in the testaments necessarily contains "God's words," meaning a direct quotation or a transcription of divine direction. Joseph taught, and his successors have emphasized, that it is the spirit of revelation within the one called of God that is the energizing force, and that in most instances God places the thought into the mind or heart of the revelator, who then assumes the

---

[4] *Teachings,* p. 327.

responsibility to clothe the oracle in language. Certainly there are times when a prophet records the words of God directly, but very often the "still small voice" (1 Kings 19:12) whispers to the prophet, who then speaks for God.

In short, an LDS view might be stated as follows: when God chooses to speak through a person, that person does not become a mindless instrument, an earthly sound system through which God can voice himself. Rather, the person becomes enlightened and filled with intelligence or truth. Nothing could be clearer in the Old Testament, for example, than that many factors affected the prophetic message—personality, experience, vocabulary, literary talent, and so on. The word of the Lord as spoken through Isaiah is quite different from the word of the Lord as spoken through Luke, and both are different from that spoken by Jeremiah or Mark. Some suggest that if the Bible cannot be trusted in all things it cannot be trusted at all. Because of the endless textual variants, some of those who believe in biblical inerrancy concede errors in our modern Bible while maintaining the infallibility of the original manuscripts. The difficulty, of course, is that the original manuscripts are no longer available.

Further, it is worth noting that stone, leaves, bark, skins, wood, metals, baked clay, and papyrus were all used anciently to record inspired messages. The LDS concern with the ancients is not the perfection with which such messages were recorded but with the inspiration of the message. More specifically, Latter-day Saints are interested in the fact that the heavens were opened to the ancients, that they had messages to record. In other words, knowing that God is the same yesterday, today, and forever (see Hebrews 13:8), the fact that he spoke to them at all, however well or poorly it may have been recorded, attests that he can speak to men and women in the here and now. After all, the Bible is only black ink on white paper until the Spirit of God manifests its true meaning to us; if we have obtained that, there is little need to quibble over the Bible's suitability as a history or science text. Perhaps a statement from Brigham Young will serve as an effective summary of the LDS view of scriptural infallibility. "When

God speaks to the people," he said, "he does it in a manner to suit their circumstances and capacities. . . . Should the Lord Almighty send an angel to re-write the Bible, it would in many places be very different from what it now is."[5]

OTHER BOOKS OF SCRIPTURE

For Joseph Smith and his followers, the traditions of the past regarding scripture, revelation, and canon were altered dramatically by the First Vision. God had spoken again, they believed, the heavens were no longer sealed, and a "new dispensation" of truth was under way. The ninth article of faith states, "We believe all that God has revealed, all that He does now reveal, and we believe that He will yet reveal many great and important things pertaining to the Kingdom of God." (Pearl of Great Price, Articles of Faith 1:9.) One writer has described the "dynamic scriptural process" of the Latter-day Saints as follows:

> Latter-day Saints hold a view of canon that does not restrict itself to God's revelations of the past, whether they be those which they revere in common with their fellow Christians or those believed uniquely by the Saints. Their view is broader: the canon is not closed, nor will it ever be. To them, revelation has not ceased; it continues in the Church. Future revelation is not only viewed as theoretically possible; it is needed and expected, as changing circumstances in the world necessitate new communication from God. This view of canon and scriptural authority is the legacy of Joseph Smith.[6]

The LDS canon of scripture, called the "standard works," consists of the Bible, the Book of Mormon, the Doctrine and Covenants, and the Pearl of Great Price.

---

[5] *Journal of Discourses* 9:311.
[6] Kent P. Jackson, "Latter-day Saints: A Dynamic Scriptural Process," in *The Holy Book in Comparative Perspective*, edited by Frederick M. Denny and Rodney L. Taylor (Columbia, South Carolina: University of South Carolina Press, 1985), p. 63.

The Book of Mormon. Over three years passed from the time of Joseph Smith's first visionary experience, and during that interim he refrained from joining any of the existing churches in the area. One evening Joseph knelt in prayer to determine his standing before God, inasmuch as he had enjoyed no further communication from God since 1820. In his own words, "On the evening of the 21st of September, A.D. 1823, while I was praying unto God, and endeavoring to exercise faith in the precious promises of Scripture, on a sudden a light like that of day, only of a far purer and more glorious appearance and brightness, burst into the room, indeed, the first sight was as though the house was filled with consuming fire; the appearance produced a shock that affected the whole body; in a moment a personage stood before me surrounded with a glory yet greater than that with which I was already surrounded."[7] The angel announced himself as Moroni and explained that "God had a work for me to do; and that my name should be had for good and evil among all nations, kindreds, and tongues, or that it should be both good and evil spoken of among all people. He said there was a book deposited, written upon gold plates, giving an account of the former inhabitants of this continent, and the source from whence they sprang. He also said that the fulness of the everlasting Gospel was contained in it, as delivered by the Savior to the ancient inhabitants." (Pearl of Great Price, Joseph Smith—History 1:33–34.) In describing the plates, as well as the manner in which he translated them, Joseph Smith said in 1842:

> These records were engraven on plates which had the appearance of gold, each plate was six inches wide and eight inches long, and not quite so thick as common tin. They were filled with engravings, in Egyptian characters, and bound together in a volume as the leaves of a book, with three rings running through the whole. The volume was something near six inches in thickness, a part of which was sealed. . . . With the records was found a curious instru-

---

[7] *History of the Church* 4:536.

ment, which the ancients called "Urim and Thummim," which consisted of two transparent stones set in the rim of a bow fastened to a breast plate. Through the medium of the Urim and Thummim I translated the record by the gift and power of God.[8]

For the Latter-day Saints, the Book of Mormon is an additional book of scripture, another testament of Jesus Christ. The majority of the Book of Mormon deals with a group of Hebrews (descendants of the tribe of Joseph, son of Jacob) who leave Jerusalem in the first year of the reign of King Zedekiah (ca. 600 B.C.), anticipating (being divinely directed concerning) the overthrow of Judah by the Babylonians. The people travel south and eventually set sail for a "promised land," a land "choice above all other lands," the land of America. The early story highlights the dissension between Nephi, a righteous and obedient leader of his people, and his rebellious and murmuring brothers, Laman and Lemuel. Prophet after prophet arises to call the people to repentance and declare the message of salvation. The Nephites are told repeatedly of the coming of Jesus, the Messiah, and the prophet leaders constantly strive to turn the hearts of the people to Christ. (The LDS belief in Christ's "eternal gospel" will be dealt with in a subsequent chapter.) Eventually the internal squabbles result in a total break of the migrants into two separate bodies of people—the followers of Nephi (Nephites) and the followers of Laman (Lamanites). The remainder of the Book of Mormon is essentially a story of the constant rise and fall of the Nephite nation (not unlike the accounts of the children of Israel contained in 2 Kings), as the people either choose to obey God or yield to the enticings of riches and pride.

The book of 3 Nephi, chapters 11–28, contains an account of a visit and brief ministry of Jesus Christ to the Nephites in America, following his death, resurrection, and ascension in the Holy Land. While teaching and comforting these "other

---

[8] Ibid., 4:537.

sheep" (John 10:14–16; Book of Mormon, 3 Nephi 15:21), Jesus organizes a church and establishes standards for a Christian community. An era of peace and unity follows for almost two hundred years as the people see to the needs of one another through having "all things in common." Later, however, the misuse of material blessings leads to pride and class distinctions, resulting in a continuation of the former struggles between good and evil. The story of the Book of Mormon culminates in a final battle between the Nephites and the Lamanites in which the former (who had proven over time to be more wicked than their idolatrous enemies) are exterminated. The history and divine dealings of the people from the time of Nephi had been kept by the prophets or civic leaders, and the final task of completing and then editing the thousand-year collection of metal plates remained for the prophet-leader Mormon (for whom the book/collection is named) and his son, Moroni, in about A.D. 400. Joseph Smith said it was this same Moroni who returned as an angel with the plates in 1823. It is, by the way, because of the Latter-day Saints' acceptance of the Book of Mormon that they have come to be known as "Mormons."

Many people in the nineteenth century claimed revelation from God, claimed visions and oracles. But the Book of Mormon made Joseph's claims somewhat different, inasmuch as it represented to many a tangible evidence of divine intervention in history. People "touched the book," as Richard Bushman has written, "and the realization came over them that God had spoken again. Apart from any specific content, the discovery of additional scripture in itself inspired faith in people who were looking for more certain evidence of God in their lives."[9] In fact, Jan Shipps observed that as important as the First Vision was to the early Saints, "it was this 'gold bible' that first attracted adherents to the movement. As crucial to the success of the whole Latter-day Saint enterprise as is Joseph Smith, it must never be forgotten that in the early years it was not the

---

[9] *Joseph Smith and the Beginnings of Mormonism* (Urbana: University of Illinois Press, 1984), p. 142.

First Vision but the Book of Mormon that provided the credentials that made the prophet's leadership so effective."[10]

The Doctrine and Covenants. Inasmuch as Joseph Smith claimed divine authority to speak for God, it was only natural that revelations and oracles given to him would be recorded. In fact, in a revelation recorded in November 1831, we find a demonstration of the broadened concept of scripture, one still held by the Latter-day Saints. This revelation stated that the elders of the Church "shall speak as they are moved upon by the Holy Ghost. And whatsoever they shall speak when moved upon by the Holy Ghost shall be scripture, shall be the will of the Lord, shall be the mind of the Lord, shall be the word of the Lord, shall be the voice of the Lord, and the power of God unto salvation." (Doctrine and Covenants 68:3–4; cited hereafter as D&C.) In 1831 the leaders of the Church began to compile the revelations received by Joseph Smith to date, and by 1833 that collection was known as *A Book of Commandments for the Government of the Church of Christ,* a volume consisting of approximately sixty-four of the present sections of the Doctrine and Covenants. Mob violence in Missouri led to the destruction of the press and the loss of all but a few copies of the Book of Commandments. In August of 1835 Joseph Smith published the first edition of the Doctrine and Covenants, an expanded form of the Book of Commandments, a collection that contained an additional forty-five revelations. Today the Doctrine and Covenants consists of 138 divisions, called "sections," and two "Official Declarations."

A perusal of the Doctrine and Covenants demonstrates that most of the revelations recorded were received during the Ohio era of the Church's history; more than twenty were received in Missouri, and fewer than ten were recorded in Illinois. In addition to the revelations through Joseph Smith, there are in the Doctrine and Covenants a revelation received by Brigham Young; a revelation to Joseph F. Smith, sixth president of the Church (1901–1918); and official declara-

---

[10] *Mormonism: The Story of a New Religious Tradition* (Urbana: University of Illinois Press, 1985), p. 33.

tions from Wilford Woodruff (fourth president, 1899–1901) and Spencer W. Kimball (twelfth president, 1973–1985).

The dynamic scriptural process of the Latter-day Saints is illustrated through a brief look at revelations added to the collection in recent years. At the April 1976 general conference of the Church, two revelations were added to the canon. One had been received by Joseph Smith in January 1836 but had never been placed in the canon. Another was received by Joseph F. Smith in October 1918. Latter-day Saints believe that both of these oracles were inspired of God—that is, they represent the will, mind, voice, and word of the Lord, even from the time they were delivered and recorded. That is, since 1836 or 1918 they were *scripture*. But in 1976 they were added to the standard works, the canon, by a vote of the Church, thus making them *canonized scripture*. As such they become binding upon the Saints, and the members of the Church are expected to read and study them and to govern their beliefs and practices according to them.

The Pearl of Great Price. In 1850 Franklin D. Richards, a young member of the Quorum of the Twelve Apostles, was called to serve as president of the British Mission of the Church. He discovered a paucity of either LDS scripture or Church literature among the Saints in England, in spite of the fact that a larger number of members resided in the British Isles at this time than in the United States. In 1851 he published a mission tract entitled *Pearl of Great Price,* a collection of various translations and narrations from Joseph Smith. Interest in and appreciation for the tract grew over the years, and by 1880 the entire Church voted to accept the Pearl of Great Price as the fourth standard work, the fourth book of scripture in the LDS canon. The Pearl of Great Price contains: (1) doctrinal details about Adam and Eve (and the Creation and Fall), Enoch, Noah, Moses, and Jesus' Olivet Discourse (Matthew 24) as made known to Joseph Smith as he undertook a serious study of the Bible; (2) more of God's dealings with Abraham; (3) an excerpt from Joseph Smith's 1838 history of the Church; and (4) thirteen statements of religious belief by Joseph Smith called the Articles of Faith.

Joseph Smith's Translation of the Bible. Though not one of the standard works of the Church, Joseph Smith's translation of the Bible is an important historical and doctrinal work of the LDS prophet. In June of 1830, just three months after the publication of the Book of Mormon, Joseph Smith began a careful study of the King James Version of the Bible and prepared what came to be known as a "new translation" of the Bible. This task he pursued actively through July 2, 1833. Working without the use of ancient languages or manuscripts, Joseph suggested changes in the text that ought to be made, according to what he felt was the spirit of revelation. Recognizing (from his work with the Book of Mormon) that many truths had been taken away or kept back from the Bible before its compilation, he set out to restore many of those things that were lost.

There was nothing particularly unusual about a new translation of the Bible in the 1830s. As discussed earlier, religious revivalism reached a peak in upstate New York in the early nineteenth century, and with it came a heightened awareness of the need for the Bible as a divine standard for living. New England was not the only section of the country that manifested an intense interest at this time in a study and scrutiny of the Bible. Records indicate that from 1777 to 1833 more than 500 separate editions of the Bible (or parts thereof) were published in America. Many of these represented new translations or "modern translations," often with an attempt to prepare paraphrased editions or alternate readings based on comparisons with Hebrew and Greek manuscripts.

Joseph Smith's "translation" was, however, quite different. Here there were no language skills and no manuscripts with which to work. Joseph believed that he had been called of God to serve as a translator, as well as a prophet, seer, and revelator. On October 8, 1829, an associate of Joseph Smith named Oliver Cowdery purchased a large pulpit-style edition of the King James Bible (containing the Old and New Testaments and Apocrypha) in Palmyra, New York. It was this Bible that was used in the translation. It appears that Joseph would read the Bible aloud and dictate alterations to a scribe who then recorded the changes on manuscript pages. In all, Joseph Smith suggested changes in at least 3,410 verses. Some of the books received more revisions than others; these were (the number indicates the number of verses that differ from the King James text):

Old Testament

Genesis (662)
Exodus (66)
Psalms (188)
Isaiah (178)

New Testament

Matthew (483)
Luke (563)
John (159)
Romans (118)
1 Corinthians (68)
Hebrews (47)
Revelation (75)

Although the most intense period of the Bible work took place between 1830 and 1833, Joseph spent the rest of his life (until 1844) preparing the manuscript for publication. In fact, the Joseph Smith Translation was never published during the Prophet's lifetime but was made available to the public in complete published form in 1867. Joseph Smith took this project very seriously and considered it to be a "branch of his calling" as prophet and restorer of the ancient order of things. Numerous revelations in the present book of Doctrine and Covenants refer to the work of translation, and Joseph Smith taught that a number of revelations came as a direct result of the Bible translation.

THE SCRIPTURES AND WORSHIP

"The sacred writings of the Latter-day Saints," observes one writer, "perform a practical function within the faith; they

SCRIPTURE AND THE EXPANDING CANON

are not used in any kind of ritual situation. They are not used in chanting, reciting, or praying, or in any similar rite . . . , nor is reading them a sacramental act. In Latter-day Saint theology the reading of scripture functions as a means to achieving an important end—education in the principles of the faith so that one can be in harmony with the will of God."[11] Latter-day Saints believe that the scriptures are to be read and searched and studied; readers of scripture are encouraged to open themselves to inspiration and to "liken the scriptures" to their own lives. In short, though the study of scripture may not be considered a sacramental act, Latter-day Saints believe that one essential key to the receipt of *individual* revelation—to know the mind and will of God in one's life—is the study of *institutional* revelation.

A modern apostle counseled Church leaders as follows: "Faith is . . . born of scriptural study. Those who study, ponder, and pray about the scriptures, seeking to understand their deep and hidden meanings, receive from time to time great outpourings of light and knowledge from the Holy Spirit. . . . However talented men may be in administrative matters; however eloquent they may be in expressing their views; however learned they may be in worldly things—they will be denied the sweet whisperings of the Spirit that might have been theirs unless they pay the price of studying, pondering, and praying about the scriptures."[12] "When this fact is admitted," Joseph Smith said in 1834, "that the immediate will of heaven is contained in the Scriptures, are we not bound as rational creatures to live in accordance to all [their] precepts?"[13]

---

[11] Jackson, "Latter-day Saints: A Dynamic Scriptural Process," p. 79.

[12] Bruce R. McConkie, in *Doctrines of the Restoration* (Salt Lake City: Bookcraft, 1989), p. 238.

[13] *Teachings,* p. 54

CHAPTER 3

GOD, MAN,
AND ANGELS

For Latter-day Saints, Joseph Smith's First Vision represents the beginning of the revelation of God in modern times. They believe that the God who manifested his will through such prophet leaders as Adam, Enoch, Noah, Abraham, and Moses appeared in a grove of trees in upstate New York in the spring of 1820. Further, they feel that the same God has continued to manifest his mind to the Church in general through living prophets and to individuals through the power of the Holy Spirit.

THE GODHEAD

Latter-day Saints worship God the Father, in the name of Christ the Son, by the power of the Holy Ghost. These three—Father, Son, and Holy Spirit—constitute the Godhead. Latter-day Saints believe that the members of the Godhead are three separate and distinct personages. Joseph Smith described them as "God the first, the Creator; God the second, the Redeemer; and God the third, the witness or Testator."[1] The

---

[1] *Teachings,* p. 190.

members of the Godhead are believed to be one in purpose, one in mind, one in glory, one in attributes and powers, but separate persons. Christ the Son and the Holy Spirit are subordinate beings to the Father, albeit divine beings, and partake of the attributes and powers of the Father. But because the second and third members of the Godhead have had extended to them the powers of the Father, because they enjoy a divine investiture of his authority, they may appropriately speak on his behalf.

God the Father. The Father is the primary personage in the Godhead. Though it is true that the term *God* is used throughout scripture (including LDS scripture) to refer to the persons or powers of Christ or the Holy Ghost, yet there is a singular and distinctive sense in which the term *God* refers to the Father. The Father is the source of light and truth, the source of all godly attributes and gifts, and the supreme intelligence over all things. Though Latter-day Saints generally refer to the Almighty as "God" or "the Lord" or "our Heavenly Father" or "Father in heaven" or simply "the Father," they also use the name-title *Elohim,* the Hebrew word used as a generic name of God. Joseph Smith taught that among the ancients God the Father was called "Man of Holiness," and thus his Only Begotten Son is known as the Son of Man of Holiness, or the Son of Man. (See Pearl of Great Price, Moses 6:57.)

It is in this context, the idea that God is a Man of Holiness, that we come upon several of the singular Latter-day Saint doctrines. First, the Latter-day Saints believe that God the Father is an exalted man, a corporeal being, a personage with flesh and bones. They do not believe he is a spirit, although they acknowledge that his Spirit or sacred influence is everywhere present. Joseph Smith taught in 1844 that God our Father was once a mortal, that he lived on an earth, died, was resurrected and glorified, and grew and developed over time to become the Almighty that he now is. To say this another way, they teach that God is all-powerful and all-knowing, but that he has not been so forever; there was once a time in an eternity past when he lived on an earth like ours. Joseph explained:

> God himself was once as we are now, and is an exalted man, and sits enthroned in yonder heavens! That is the great secret. If the veil were rent today, and the great God who holds this world in its orbit, and who upholds all worlds and all things by his power, was to make himself visible—I say, if you were to see him today, you would see him like a man in form—like yourselves in all the person, image, and very form as a man. . . . It is the first principle of the Gospel to know for a certainty the character of God, and to know that we may converse with him as one man converses with another, and that he was once a man like us; yea, that God himself, the Father of us all, dwelt on an earth, the same as Jesus Christ himself did.[2]

When considering how the rest of the Christian world views God, these things surely appear strange and unusual. The Latter-day Saints do not doubt that God has power to know all that needs to be known and to do whatever is possible to be done. They believe in a being in whom they can trust implicitly and with whom they can identify. For them, God is not simply an essence, a spirit influence, a force in the universe, the Prime Mover, or the First Great Cause; when they pray, as did Jesus, "Our Father which art in heaven" (Matthew 6:9), they mean what they say. They believe that God is not outside time, that he is approachable and knowable, and that, like his Beloved Son, he can be touched with the feeling of our infirmities (Hebrews 4:15).

Jesus Christ. We will consider in more detail in a later chapter the LDS view of Christ's atonement and the way salvation comes to men and women through him. For now we will simply speak broadly of the person and work of Jesus. Latter-day Saints believe that Jesus the Christ is the same being as Jehovah (Yahweh), the God of the ancients, the God of Abraham, Isaac, and Jacob; that under the direction of the

---

[2] Ibid., pp. 345–46.

Father he created the worlds (see John 1:3; Ephesians 3:9; Hebrews 1:2); that as an act of mercy and grace, an act of supreme condescension, Jehovah came to earth and took a body of flesh and bones and became Jesus of Nazareth.

Latter-day Saints teach that Jesus of Nazareth was and is the Son of God, the Savior and Redeemer of the world. As Ezra Taft Benson, thirteenth president of the Church, has written, "The Church of Jesus Christ of Latter-day Saints proclaims that Jesus Christ is the Son of God in the most literal sense. The body in which He performed His mission in the flesh was sired by that same Holy Being we worship as God, our Eternal Father. Jesus was not the son of Joseph, nor was He begotten by the Holy Ghost. He is the Son of the Eternal Father."[3] The Saints teach that Mary was Jesus' mother and God was his Father. From Mary Jesus inherited mortality, the capacity to die. From God he inherited immortality, the capacity to live forever. His sufferings and death were a willing sacrifice, and no man took his life from him. Jesus thus had the capacity to die and the power to rise from death and live forever. (See John 10:18.)

There is no question among believing Latter-day Saints but that Jesus was divine. Let me say that another way. In this interesting age wherein scholars continue to debate what Jesus "really" said and did, Latter-day Saints have no problem accepting that the Jesus of history is indeed the Christ of faith. They see no need to doubt the united testimonies of the Gospel writers or to assume that the examples in the New Testament of visions, dreams, healings, predictive prophecies, or divine interventions were anything other than what they are described to be. The Church of Jesus Christ of Latter-day Saints has at the core of its teachings the unshakable conviction that Jesus was the Son of God, that he lived, taught, suffered, died, rose from the dead, and lives again, and that because he lives we shall live also.

The Holy Ghost. Although the Father and the Son are beings of flesh and bones (albeit resurrected and glorified

---

[3] *Come unto Christ* (Salt Lake City: Deseret Book Co., 1983), p. 4.

flesh and bones), the Holy Ghost or Holy Spirit is a personage of spirit, a spirit man. Heber C. Kimball, one of the early leaders of the Church, explained that "the Holy Ghost is a man; he is one of the sons of our Father and our God."[4] Joseph Smith likewise taught that "the Holy Ghost is yet a spiritual body and waiting to take to himself a [physical] body."[5] He is the messenger of the Father and the Son, the Comforter, the Witness or Testator. Some of his roles include: (1) to comfort in times of distress or uncertainty, to bring peace to the troubled soul; (2) to bring things to remembrance; (3) to reveal the things of God, to make known matters that can be known and understood only through faith, to bear witness of the truth; (4) to sanctify, to purify the human heart, to purge men and women of sins and of sinfulness.

THE NATURE OF MAN

Latter-day Saints believe that Adam and Eve were real people, our first parents, and that they lived in the Garden of Eden. The LDS view of the scenes in Eden are remarkably optimistic when compared to the traditional Catholic or Protestant views. Mormons believe that Adam and Eve went into the Garden to fall, that their partaking of the forbidden fruit was a necessary step in God's plan for the redemption and happiness of humankind. Though our first parents transgressed the law of God, their partaking opened the way to mortality, to trial and testing to be sure, but to happiness that comes from overcoming. As stated in the Book of Mormon, "Adam fell that men might be; and men are, that they might have joy." (2 Nephi 2:25.) Joseph Smith explained, "We believe that men will be punished for their own sins, and not for Adam's transgression." (Pearl of Great Price, Articles of Faith 1:2.) From the above, Latter-day Saints conclude the following:

---

[4] *Journal of Discourses* 5:179.
[5] *Words of Joseph Smith,* edited by Andrew F. Ehat and Lyndon W. Cook (Provo: BYU Religious Studies Center, 1980), p. 382; punctuation corrected.

1. Adam's transgression in Eden was forgiven, and thus there is no "original sin" or guilt or taint entailed upon Adam and Eve's posterity. For that reason, baptism is only for those who are accountable morally for their deeds and who are in a position to have faith in Christ and repent of their sins. Latter-day Saints do not believe that children are capable of sin; that is, whatever children under the age of eight years (the age of accountability) may do that is inappropriate or otherwise sinful is covered by the atonement of Jesus. Parents are responsible to teach their children the principles of faith, repentance, baptism, and the need for the Holy Ghost by the time the children arrive at the years of accountability; if they do not, the sins of the children rest upon the heads of their parents. (D&C 68:25–28.)

2. Latter-day Saints do not believe in the depravity of men and women. They believe men and women have the power to choose good. But they do believe in the effects of the Fall. That is, though they do not believe children are "born in sin"—that sin entails upon children because of what Adam and Eve did or what the children's parents did—LDS scripture does suggest that children are "conceived in sin." (Pearl of Great Price, Moses 6:55.) First, we are conceived into a world of sin. Second, conception becomes the vehicle, the means whereby a fallen nature—mortality, "the flesh," as described by the Apostle Paul—is transmitted to the descendants of Adam and Eve. To say this another way, Latter-day Saint scripture teaches that the seeds of death and sin are present in conception. A child is neither sinful nor dead when born, but the seeds of both are present. Just as one moves toward death each day he or she lives, so also the capacity to sin is present from the time one arrives at the age of accountability. One aspect of the atonement of Jesus is thus redemption from a nature that longs to sin, a nature that tends toward spiritual dissolution.

3. Men and women have the choice, the moral agency, to yield either to the persuasions of the world or to the enticings of the Holy Spirit. Those who choose the former enter the realm of sin and, without repentance, in time surrender their

will to that of Satan. Those who choose the latter, who decide to put off the "natural man" (see 1 Corinthians 2:11–14) and put on Christ through the Atonement, open themselves to change and renewal. Through repentance—through turning away from their old ways and surrendering to the mind of God through the Holy Spirit—these become "new creatures in Christ," men and women who die to the old ways of sin and are born again to the ways of righteousness. This is a prominent teaching in the Book of Mormon: "The Messiah cometh in the fulness of time, that he may redeem the children of men from the fall. And because that they are redeemed from the fall they have become free forever, knowing good from evil; to act for themselves and not to be acted upon. . . . Wherefore, men are free according to the flesh; and all things are given them which are expedient unto man. And they are free to choose liberty and eternal life, through the great Mediator of all men, or to choose captivity and death." (Book of Mormon, 2 Nephi 2:26–27.) Or, as another passage explains: "And now remember, remember, . . . that whosoever perisheth, perisheth unto himself; and whosoever doeth iniquity, doeth it unto himself; for behold, ye are free; ye are permitted to act for yourselves." (Book of Mormon, Helaman 14:30.)

In a later chapter we will deal with the LDS view that men and women are the sons and daughters of God; that we are of the same species as God; that there is an element of godliness within each of us; and that we thus have the capacity to become like God. (See chapter 14, question 20; appendix 2, "Distinctive LDS Doctrines.") Further, we will attend to the matter of the spirit of man and its relationship to the physical body. For now, let it be stated that there is no pat, settled view on the nature of man. Is he good by nature? Is she depraved by nature? It depends upon what man or woman we are speaking of. If he has yielded to sin and refuses to repent and return to God, then it could be said that he is a natural man, an enemy to God and to things of godliness. If, on the other hand, she has fallen into sin but determines upon a course of sincere repentance, she is on the path to peace and happiness. The real issue is whether a man or woman, a being of moral agency, is moving toward or away from God and divinity. "We have to fight continually," Brigham Young observed, "as it were, sword in hand to make the spirit master of the tabernacle, or the flesh subject to the law of the spirit. If this warfare is not diligently prosecuted, then the law of sin prevails. . . . The rule of the flesh brings darkness and death, while, on the other hand, the rule of the [Holy] Spirit brings light and life."[6]

Latter-day Saints believe that although people can be changed and renewed in Christ, yet the pull upon the human system from mortality and the Fall will be ever with us. There can come a time when people have no more disposition to do evil but to do good continually (see Book of Mormon, Mosiah 5:2), when they feel an abhorrence for sinful things (Book of Mormon, Alma 13:12), when they shake at the very appearance of sin (Book of Mormon, 2 Nephi 4:31). But until mortality is ended, people will continue to be tempted, to be pained by the allurements of a sinful environment. Brigham Young said, "It requires all the atonement of Christ, the mercy of the Father, the pity of angels and the grace of the Lord Jesus Christ to be with us always, and then to do the very best we possibly can, to get rid of this sin within us."[7] "Will sin be perfectly destroyed?" he asked on another occasion.

> No, it will not, for it is not so designed in the economy of heaven. . . . Do not suppose that we shall ever be free from temptations to sin. Some suppose that they can in the flesh be sanctified body and spirit and become so pure that they will never again feel the effects of the power of the adversary of truth. Were it possible for a person to attain to this degree of perfection in the flesh, he could not die neither remain in a world where sin predominates. . . . I think we shall more or less feel the effects of sin so long as we live, and finally have to pass the ordeals of death.[8]

---

[6] *Journal of Discourses* 9:287–88.
[7] Ibid., 11:301.
[8] Ibid., 10:173.

The Latter-day Saints believe that the physical body is a blessing, not something to be shunned or detested. In fact, although men and women can enjoy the peace and happiness associated with faithfulness in this life, a "fulness of joy" can come only after body and spirit have been reunited in the resurrection. (See D&C 93:33–34.) "Our bodies are important to us," Brigham Young stated, "though they may be old and withered,

> emaciated with toil, pain, and sickness, and our limbs bent with rheumatism, all uniting to hasten dissolution, for death is sown in our mortal bodies. The foods we partake of are contaminated with the seeds of death, yet we partake of them to extend our lives until our allotted work is finished, when our tabernacles in a state of ripeness are sown in the earth to produce immortal fruit. Yet if we live our holy religion and let the spirit reign, it will not become dull and stupid, but as the body approaches dissolution the spirit [of man] takes a firmer hold on the enduring substance behind the veil, drawing from the depth of that eternal Fountain of Light sparkling gems of intelligence which surround the frail and sinking tabernacle with a halo of immortal wisdom.[9]

GOD, MAN, AND ABSOLUTE TRUTH

Joseph Smith and his successors in the presidency of the Church have consistently instructed the Saints that truth is fixed, eternal, and undeviating. "Truth is knowledge of things as they are, and as they were, and as they are to come." (D&C 93:24.) Truth is not established by consensus, by popular vote, or by utility alone. Likewise, right and wrong are not defined by society. Latter-day Saints believe in absolute truths. They believe that because God's laws are constant and consistent, people may depend with certainty upon the consequences of obedience and disobedience.

---

[9] Ibid., 9:288.

Perhaps one of the clearest statements by a Church leader on this subject was an address delivered at Brigham Young University in 1977 by Spencer W. Kimball, twelfth president of the Church. His address was based upon a letter he had written to a young man whose faith had faltered because of his doubts.

> God, our Heavenly Father—Elohim—lives. That is an absolute truth. All four billion of the children of men on the earth might be ignorant of him and his attributes and his powers, but he still lives. All the people on the earth might deny him and disbelieve, but he lives in spite of them. They may have their own opinions, but he still lives, and his form, powers, and attributes do not change according to men's opinions. In short, opinion alone has no power in the matter of an absolute truth. He still lives. And Jesus Christ is the Son of God, the Almighty, the Creator, the Master of the only true way of life—the gospel of Jesus Christ. The intellectual may rationalize him out of existence and the unbeliever may scoff, but Christ lives and guides the destinies of his people. That is an absolute truth; there is no gainsaying.
>
> The watchmaker in Switzerland, with materials at hand, made the watch that was found in the sand in a California desert. The people who found the watch had never been to Switzerland, nor seen the watchmaker, nor seen the watch made. The watchmaker still existed, no matter the extent of their ignorance or experience. If the watch had a tongue, it might even lie and say, "There is no watchmaker." That would not alter the truth.

"If men are really humble," President Kimball added, "they will realize that they discover, but do not create, truth."[10]

It is an understanding of the constancy of God's laws, as well as the knowledge of God's perfections, that enables men and women to exercise faith in God unto salvation. The early

---

[10] "Absolute Truth," *1977 BYU Speeches of the Year* (Provo: BYU Publications, 1978), p. 138.

leaders of the Church stressed that without the confidence that God has all power, knows all things, and is perfectly just, truthful, and merciful, it is impossible to trust in him sufficient to attain heaven. To believe otherwise, Joseph Smith taught, is to live without true faith, to live in doubt of God's powers and might, to fear that perhaps there might be one greater than He. "Without the knowledge of all things, God would not be able to save any portion of his creatures; for it is by reason of the knowledge which he has of all things, from the beginning to the end, that enables him to give that understanding to his creatures by which they are made partakers of eternal life; and if it were not for the idea existing in the minds of men that God had all knowledge it would be impossible for them to exercise faith in him."[11]

ANGELS

Few things have gripped the United States like the recent craze over angels. Hundreds of books, lectures, movies, and television shows have come before the public possessing one common element—the involvement of angels in the lives of ordinary men and women. There are songs about angels, angel bookmarks, and in some cases designated experts who speak at length of how to encourage and benefit from the ministry of angels. Some religious leaders are concerned that angel mania has led many of their congregants to unwise and excessive measures, while the more cynical in our midst are somewhat amused by what they perceive to be massive gullibility.

C. S. Lewis, writing of the reality of demons, observed, "There are two equal and opposite errors into which our race can fall about the devils. One is to disbelieve in their existence. The other is to believe, and to feel an excessive and unhealthy interest in them. They themselves are equally pleased by both errors, and hail a materialist or a magician with the same delight."[12] This principle holds for Latter-day

---

[11] *Lectures on Faith* (Salt Lake City: Deseret Book Co., 1995), 4:11.

[12] *The Screwtape Letters,* rev. ed. (New York: Macmillan, 1982), p. 3.

Saints in regard to angels as well as devils. The Latter-day Saints are not caught up in the angel craze, no doubt because the concept of the ministry of angels is so fundamentally crucial to the fabric of their faith to begin with. The Church claims to have begun with the ministry of angels and that this is one of the means whereby the Almighty communicates his mind and will to his children. Mormonism claims to be the fulfillment of a prophecy concerning the coming of an angel: "I saw another angel fly in the midst of heaven, having the everlasting gospel to preach unto them that dwell on the earth, and to every nation, and kindred, and tongue, and people." (Revelation 14:6.)

Latter-day Saints believe that angels are men and women, human beings, sons and daughters of God, personages of the same type as we are. Parley P. Pratt, an early apostle, wrote, "Gods, angels and men are all of one species, one race, one great family."[13] Elder Bruce R. McConkie, a more recent apostle, wrote, "These messengers, agents, angels of the Almighty, are chosen from among his offspring and are themselves pressing forward along the course of progression and salvation, all in their respective spheres."[14] In spite of prevailing sentiments in the religious world, as well as in Christian traditions and legends, Joseph Smith taught that angels do not have wings.[15] These beings, Joseph explained, either have lived or will live on this earth at some time in its history. (D&C 130:5.) They do minister to people on earth, sometimes being seen and often unseen. They are subject to the will and power of Jesus Christ. (Moroni 7:30.) Further, there are various kinds of angels, including:

• *Unembodied spirits.* Latter-day Saints believe that on some occasions angels have appeared who are unembodied spirits, men and women who have not yet taken a physical body through birth. The Bible speaks of the war in heaven in which "Michael and his angels" fought against Lucifer.

---

[13] *Key to the Science of Theology* [Salt Lake City: Deseret Book Co., 1978], p. 21.

[14] *Mormon Doctrine*, 2nd ed. [Salt Lake City: Bookcraft, 1966], p. 35.

[15] *Teachings*, p. 162.

(Revelation 12:7.) In LDS scripture, a story is told of Adam and Eve, after their expulsion from Eden but presumably before anyone had died, being commanded to worship God and to "offer the firstlings of their flocks, for an offering unto the Lord." They obeyed. "And after many days an angel of the Lord appeared unto Adam, saying: Why dost thou offer sacrifices unto the Lord? And Adam said unto him: I know not, save the Lord commanded me. And then the angel spake, saying: This thing is a similitude of the sacrifice of the Only Begotten of the Father, which is full of grace and truth. Wherefore, thou shalt do all that thou doest in the name of the Son, and thou shalt repent and call upon God in the name of the Son forevermore." (Pearl of Great Price, Moses 5:5–8.) Latter-day Saints believe that Michael the Archangel later became the man Adam, while Gabriel was born into the world as Noah.[16]

• *Disembodied spirits.* Those who have completed their work on earth, have passed through death, and are now part of the postmortal spirit world may be sent to minister to mortals. Those who are called "just men [or women] made perfect" have not yet been resurrected but will yet receive a celestial resurrection. (Hebrews 12:22–24; D&C 129:3.)

• *Resurrected beings.* The scriptures record that when Jesus rose from the tomb, other Saints did the same; these resurrected beings ministered for a season to friends and loved ones. (Matthew 27:52–53; see also Book of Mormon, Helaman 14:25.) These, having bodies of flesh and bones, are able to minister in ways that spirits cannot. Such beings, like the risen Lord on the road to Emmaus, are able to shield their glory when they appear to mortals. (Luke 24:13–35.)[17]

• *Mortals.* There is a limited sense in which mortal men and women may assist God in bringing to pass the salvation of his sons and daughters. The Almighty can inspire good people to lift and lighten burdens and thus to liberate those who may be struggling with personal problems.

---

[16] Ibid., p. 157.
[17] See also *Teachings*, p. 325.

Angels enjoy a measure of the Spirit and power of God and can represent him in many ways, including: (1) Teaching and testifying of the truth or calling people to repentance. (2) Warning and delivering from peril. (3) Comforting and reassuring. (4) Serving as destroying angels. (5) Conferring divine authority and power. As the episode in Acts 9 concerning the call of Saul of Tarsus suggests, angels do not do for mortals what mortals could do for themselves.[18] Latter-day Saints believe, for example, that the love and tender regard parents have for their children do not cease when death separates the family for a season. One Church leader explained:

> I believe we move and have our being in the presence of heavenly messengers and of heavenly beings. We are not separate from them. We begin to realize, more and more fully, as we become acquainted with the principles of the gospel, as they have been revealed anew in this dispensation, that we are closely related to our kindred, to our ancestors, to our friends and associates and co-laborers who have preceded us into the spirit world. We can not forget them; we do not cease to love them; we always hold them in our hearts, in memory. . . . How much more certain it is and reasonable and consistent to believe that those who have been faithful, who have gone beyond and are still engaged in the work for the salvation of the souls of men, . . . can see us better than we can see them; that they know us better than we know them. They have advanced; we are advancing; we are growing as they have grown; we are reaching the goal that they have attained unto; and therefore, I claim that we live in their presence, they see us, they are solicitous for our welfare, they love us now more than ever. For now they see the dangers that beset us; they can comprehend, better than ever before, the weaknesses that are liable to mislead us into dark and forbidden paths. They see the temptations and the evils that beset us in life and the proneness of mortal beings to yield to temptation and to do wrong; hence their solicitude for us, and their love for

---

[18] See *Teachings*, p. 265.

us, and their desire for our well being, must be greater than that which we feel for ourselves.[19]

In all of this there is no sensationalism, no aberrations, no encouragement from Church leaders to reach beyond the bounds of propriety in seeking to communicate or associate with those in the spirit world. Latter-day Saints believe there is order in the government of the kingdom of God and that heavenly messengers minister according to the will of God, not whim or fancy, either on the part of mortals or angels. Angels of God may thus not be conjured or somehow compelled by mortals to do their bidding. Angels are part of the divine program of Deity. Their reality attests to the significant truth that mortals are not alone, that we need not fear, for, in the language of the Old Testament prophet, "they that be with us are more than they that be with them." (2 Kings 6:16.)

[19] Joseph F. Smith, "In the Presence of the Divine," in *Messages of the First Presidency,* 6 vols., compiled by James R. Clark (Salt Lake City: Bookcraft, 1965–75), 5:6–7.

CHAPTER 4

JESUS CHRIST AND THE PLAN OF SALVATION

L atter-day Saints believe there is purpose in life, that there are things to be felt and experienced and accomplished in this existence that bring peace and contentment; there are other attitudes and actions that lead to misery and despair. The Latter-day Saints hold tenaciously to the principle that God our Father has a plan for us. The plan—called variously the plan of salvation, the plan of redemption, the great plan of happiness—serves as a guide, a roadmap of sorts, through trying and confusing and even ironic circumstances in life. In this chapter we will focus on the vital role of Jesus Christ in that plan of salvation.

AN ETERNAL GOSPEL

Latter-day Saints have a rather unusual view of Christianity. They believe that Christian doctrines have been taught and Christian sacraments administered by Christian prophets since the beginning of time. Adam and Eve were Christians. Noah warned the people in his day to repent, believe, and be baptized in the name of Jesus Christ. Abraham and Moses and Isaiah and Jeremiah and Ezekiel were Christian prophets.

If all of this seems odd, anachronistic in the sense that there could obviously be no Christianity until the coming to earth of the Christ, Latter-day Saints believe otherwise. They believe and teach that among the plain and precious truths lost from the holy records that became the Bible is the knowledge of Christ's eternal gospel, the message that a gospel or plan of salvation was had from the dawn of time. In this sense, the Latter-day Saints do not accept a developmental or evolutionary approach to the New Testament. They do not accept the view that the antediluvians, for example, were primitives or that the so-called Christian era we generally associate with the birth or ministry of Jesus is in some way superior, on a higher plane, or more spiritually advanced than the eras of the Old Testament patriarchs or prophets. It is true that the Latter-day Saints speak of the Christian era as "the meridian of time," but this has reference to the centrality of Christ's ministry, teachings, and atoning sacrifice more than to the uniqueness of the message delivered in the first century.

Latter-day Saints believe that God has revealed himself and his plan of salvation during different periods of the earth's history; these periods are known as *dispensations.* The Adamic dispensation was the first. LDS scripture declares that Adam and Eve, after their expulsion from the Garden of Eden, called upon God in prayer and came to know the course in life they should pursue through God's voice, by the ministry of angels, and by revelation through the power of the Holy Ghost. They then taught the gospel to their children and grandchildren, and thus the knowledge of God, of a coming Savior, and of a plan for the redemption and reclamation of wandering souls was in effect early on. (See Pearl of Great Price, Moses 5:1–8.) From the Pearl of Great Price comes the following counsel of God to Adam: "[God] called upon our father Adam by his own voice, saying: I am God; I made the world, and men before they were in the flesh. And he also said unto him: If thou wilt turn unto me, and hearken unto my voice, and believe, and repent of all thy transgressions, and be baptized, even in water, in the name of mine Only

Begotten Son, who is full of grace and truth, which is Jesus Christ, the only name which shall be given under heaven, whereby salvation shall come unto the children of men, ye shall receive the gift of the Holy Ghost." (Moses 6:51–52.) Adam was further instructed to teach his children of the necessity for spiritual rebirth, that by "transgression cometh the fall, which fall bringeth death, and inasmuch as ye were born into the world by water, and blood, and the spirit, which I have made, and so became of dust a living soul, even so ye must be born again into the kingdom of heaven, of water, and of the Spirit, and be cleansed by blood, even the blood of mine Only Begotten." (Moses 6:59.)

Other dispensations followed, periods of time wherein the heavens were opened, prophets were called and empowered, and new truths and new authorities were restored to the earth, usually following a time of falling away or apostasy. Thus the ministries and teachings of Enoch, Noah, Abraham, Moses, Jesus, and Joseph Smith introduced major dispensations, periods wherein God—his person and plan—was revealed anew. Lest there be misunderstanding at this point, I hasten to add that Jesus Christ is chief, preeminent, and supreme over all the prophets. Latter-day Saints would acknowledge Jesus as a prophet, a restorer, a revealer of God, but more than this, they stand firm in attesting to his divinity. While the prophets were called of God, Jesus *is* God. He is the Son of God. Under the Father, his is the power by which men and women are forgiven, redeemed, and born again to a new spiritual life. LDS scriptures teach that all the prophets from the beginning testified of Christ—that all of those called as spokesmen or mouthpieces for God were, first and foremost, witnesses of the Redeemer, inasmuch as "the testimony of Jesus is the spirit of prophecy." (Revelation 19:10.) In the words of Peter, to Christ "give all the prophets witness." (Acts 10:43; see also 1 Peter 1:10–11.)

In the Book of Mormon, one of the prophet leaders, living in about 73 B.C., explains to his son, "Behold, you marvel why these things"—the coming atonement of Jesus of Nazareth—"should be known so long beforehand. Behold, I say unto you, is not a soul at this time as precious unto God as a soul will be at the time of his coming? Is it not as necessary that the plan of redemption should be made known unto this people as well as unto their children? Is it not as easy at this time for the Lord to send his angel to declare these glad tidings unto us as unto our children, or as after the time of his coming?" (Alma 39:17–19.) In that same vein, Joseph Smith recorded the following in April of 1830:

> The Almighty God gave his Only Begotten Son, as it is written in those scriptures which have been given of him. He suffered temptations but gave no heed unto them. He was crucified, died, and rose again the third day; and ascended into heaven, to sit down on the right hand of the Father . . . ; that as many as would believe and be baptized in his holy name, and endure in faith to the end, should be saved—*not only those who believed after he came in the meridian of time, in the flesh, but all those from the beginning, even as many as were before he came, who believed in the words of the holy prophets, who spake as they were inspired by the gift of the Holy Ghost, who truly testified of him in all things, should have eternal life, as well as those who should come after,* who should believe in the gifts and callings of God by the Holy Ghost, which beareth record of the Father and of the Son. (D&C 20:21–27; emphasis added.)

The fullness of the gospel plan, the covenant between God and humankind, is thus known as the new and everlasting covenant. It is *new* in the sense that it is new to those to whom it is restored and revealed; it is *everlasting* in the sense that it has been around for a long, long time. We will speak in some detail of the nature of the covenant in a later chapter. For now, let us quote briefly from Joseph Smith on the eternal nature of the gospel covenant:

> Perhaps our friends will say that the Gospel and its ordinances were not known till the days of John, the son of Zacharias, in the days of Herod, the king of Judea.

But we will here look at this point: For our own part
we cannot believe that the ancients in all ages were so
ignorant of the system of heaven as many suppose, since all
that were ever saved, were saved through the power of this
great plan of redemption, as much before the coming of
Christ as since; if not, God has had different plans in operation (if we may so express it), to bring men back to dwell
with Himself; and this we cannot believe, since there has
been no change in the constitution of man since he fell. . . .
It will be noticed that, according to Paul (see Galatians 3:8)
the Gospel was preached to Abraham. We would like to be
informed in what name the Gospel was then preached,
whether it was in the name of Christ or some other name. If
in any other name, was it the Gospel? And if it was the Gospel, and that preached in the name of Christ, had it any
ordinances [sacraments]? If not, was it the Gospel?[1]

To say this another way, Latter-day Saints teach that the
knowledge of a Savior and the plan of salvation have been
revealed throughout history, and not simply since the mortal
ministry of Jesus of Nazareth. This may be one reason why so
many elements common to Christianity, remnants of a primitive Christian message—a god becoming a man, a virgin birth,
the sacrifice of a god, and so on—are to be found in cultures
far and wide, even dating well before the birth of Jesus. As
Joseph F. Smith, nephew of the Prophet Joseph and himself
sixth president of the Church, explained, "When I read books
that are scattered broadcast through the world, throwing dis-
credit upon words and teachings and doctrines of the Lord
Jesus Christ, saying that some of the ideas Jesus uttered,
truths that he promulgated, have been enunciated before by
the ancient philosophers among the heathen nations of the
world, I want to tell you that there is not a heathen philosopher that ever lived in all the world from the beginning, that
had a truth or enunciated a principle of God's truth that did

___
[1] *Teachings*, pp. 59–60.

not receive it from the fountain head, from God himself."[2] On another occasion he stated:

> Let it be remembered that Christ was with the Father from the beginning, that the gospel of truth and light existed from the beginning, and is from everlasting to everlasting. The Father, Son, and Holy Ghost, as one God, are the fountain of truth. From this fountain all the ancient learned philosophers have received their inspiration and wisdom—from it they have received all their knowledge. If we find truth in broken fragments through the ages, it may be set down as an incontrovertible fact that it originated at the fountain, and was given to philosophers, inventors, patriots, reformers, and prophets by the inspiration of God. It came from him through his Son Jesus Christ and the Holy Ghost, in the first place, and from no other source. It is eternal.
>
> Christ, therefore, being the fountain of truth, is no imitator. He taught the truth first; it was his before it was given to man. When he came to the earth he not only proclaimed new thought, but repeated some of the everlasting principles which had been heretofore only partly understood and enunciated by the wisest of men. And in so doing he enlarged in every instance upon the wisdom which they had originally received from him, because of his superior abilities and wisdom, and his association with the Father and the Holy Ghost. He did not imitate men. They made known in their imperfect way what the inspiration of Jesus Christ had taught them, for they obtained their enlightenment first from him.[3]

THE ATONEMENT OF CHRIST

Gospel means "good news" or "glad tidings." The bad news is that because of the fall of our first parents we are subject to the effects and pull of sin and death. The bad news is that because of the fall men and women experience spiritual

---

[2] *Gospel Doctrine* (Salt Lake City: Deseret Book Co., 1971), p. 395.
[3] Ibid., pp. 398–99.

death—separation and alienation from the presence and influence of God and of things of righteousness. The bad news is that every man, woman, and child will one day face the grim reaper, the universal horror we know as physical death. The good news is that there is help, relief, extrication from the pain and penalty of our sins. The good news is that there is reconciliation with God the Father through the mediation of his Son, Jesus Christ. The good news is that there is an atonement, literally an at-one-ment with the Father. The good news is that the victory of the grave and the sting of death are swallowed up in the power of One greater than death. (1 Corinthians 15:54–55; see also Isaiah 25:8.) The good news is the promise of eventual life after death through the resurrection. In short, the gospel is the good news that Christ came to earth, lived and taught and suffered and died and rose again, all to the end that those who believe and obey might be delivered from death and sin unto eternal life. This good news Latter-day Saints have in common with Christians throughout the world.

Latter-day Saints believe that Jesus was and is a perfect man, that he did what no other man or woman has ever done—he lived a perfect life. He was tempted in all points just as we are, but he did not yield. (Hebrews 4:15; 1 Peter 2:22.) Jesus was the truth and he taught the truth, and his teachings stand as a formula for happiness, a guide for personal, inter-personal, and world peace. His messages, as contained in the New Testament, are timely and timeless; they are a treasure house of wisdom and divine direction for our lives. Other men and women have spoken the truth, offered wise counsel for our lives, and even provided profound insight as to who we are and what life is all about. But Jesus did what no other person could do—he atoned for our sins and rose from the dead. Only a god, only a person with power over death, could do such things.

Mormons teach that the atonement of Christ began in the Garden of Gethsemane and was consummated on the cross of Calvary. His sufferings, as described in the four Gospels, rep-resented far more than the anticipation and fear of the cross, although no sane person would do other than dread such a cruel fate. Rather, his sufferings in the Garden—including sweating blood (Luke 22:44)—came because of his agony for the sins of the world. One of the direct consequences of sin is the withdrawal of the Father's Spirit, resulting in feelings of loss, anxiety, disappointment, fear, alienation, and guilt. Latter-day Saint scripture and prophet leaders affirm that Jesus experienced the withdrawal of the Father's Spirit and thus suffered in both body and spirit.[4] The withdrawal of the Spirit lasted for a period of hours in Gethsemane and reoccurred on the cross the next day. It was for this reason that Jesus cried out, "My God, my God, why hast thou forsaken me?" (Matthew 27:46.) A Book of Mormon prophet described our Lord's sufferings as follows: "He cometh into the world that he may save all men if they will hearken unto his voice; for behold, he suffereth the pains of all men, yea, the pains of every living creature, both men, women, and children, who belong to the family of Adam." (2 Nephi 9:21.) Another Nephite leader explained, "He shall suffer temptations, and pain of body, hunger, thirst, and fatigue, even more than man can suffer, except it be unto death; for behold, blood cometh from every pore, so great shall be his anguish for the wickedness and the abominations of his people." (Mosiah 3:7.)

How this atonement took place is unknown. The Latter-day Saints believe in Christ and trust in his redeeming mercy and grace. They accept the word of scripture, both ancient and modern, in regard to the ransoming mission of Jesus the Christ. They know from personal experience—having been transformed from pain to peace, from darkness to light—of the power in Christ to renew the human soul. But, like the rest of the Christian world, they cannot rationally conceive the work of a God. They cannot grasp how one man can assume the effect of another man's error, and, more especially, how one man, even a man possessed of the power of God the Father, can suffer for another's sins. The atonement,

---

[4] See D&C 19:15–20; Brigham Young, *Journal of Discourses* 3:205–6.

the greatest act of mercy and love in all eternity, though real, is, for now, incomprehensible and unfathomable.

In a subsequent chapter we will discuss the LDS view of the premortal and postmortal nature of men and women. For now, let us simply observe that physical death is the separation of spirit and body. Following death, the spirit goes into a spirit world to await the time when spirit and body are reunited, the time we know as the resurrection. Latter-day Saints accept the account in the New Testament that Jesus of Nazareth died on the cross, was taken down by his disciples, and was placed in a tomb. On the third day he rose from the dead. His physical body was joined again with his spirit. With that physical body he walked and talked and taught and ate and ministered. The resurrection of Jesus is of monumental importance; it was the first occurrence of a resurrection and stands as a physical proof of the divine Sonship of Jesus. Again, in a way that is incomprehensible to finite minds, the LDS people believe, as do Christians everywhere, that Christ's rising from the tomb opened the door for all men and women to rise one day from death to life. In short, because he rose, we shall also, in the proper time: "He cometh unto his own, that salvation might come unto the children of men even through faith on his name; and even after all this they shall consider him a man, and say that he hath a devil, and shall scourge him, and shall crucify him. And he shall rise the third day from the dead." (Book of Mormon, Mosiah 3:9–10.) Also: "If Christ had not come into the world . . . , there could have been no redemption. And if Christ had not risen from the dead, or have broken the bands of death that the grave should have no victory, and that death should have no sting, there could have been no resurrection. But there is a resurrection, therefore the grave hath no victory, and the sting of death is swallowed up in Christ. He is the light and the life of the world; yea, a light that is endless, that can never be darkened; yea, and also a life which is endless, that there can be no more death." (Book of Mormon, Mosiah 16:6–9.)

In the Pearl of Great Price are recorded the following words of God to Moses the Lawgiver: "This is my work and my glory—to bring to pass the immortality and eternal life of man." (Pearl of Great Price, Moses 1:39.) This is a capsule statement, a succinct summary of the work of redemption in Christ. Latter-day Saints believe there are two types of salvation made available through the atonement of Jesus Christ— universal and individual. All who take a physical body—good or bad, evil or righteous—will be resurrected. That is, all will one day rise from death to life, their spirits reuniting with their bodies, never again to be divided. "As in Adam all die, even so in Christ shall all be made alive." (1 Corinthians 15:22.) This is universal salvation. It is salvation from physical death, a salvation available to all. *Immortality* is salvation from the grave. It is endless life. It is a universal gift.

Individual salvation is another matter. Though all salvation is available through the goodness and grace of Christ, Latter-day Saints believe there are certain things that must be done in order for divine grace and mercy to be activated in the lives of individual followers of Christ. We must come unto him—accept him as Lord and Savior, have faith on his name, repent of sin, be baptized, receive the gift of the Holy Ghost, and strive to keep God's commandments to the end of our days. *Eternal life,* known also as salvation or exaltation, comes to those who believe and seek to remain true to the gospel covenant. Christ is "the author of eternal salvation unto all them that obey him." (Hebrews 5:9.) One Book of Mormon prophet thus observed, "[Christ] shall come into the world to redeem his people; and he shall take upon him the transgressions of those who believe on his name; and these are they that shall have eternal life, and salvation cometh to none else. Therefore the wicked remain as though there had been no redemption made, except it be the loosing of the bands of death; for behold, the day cometh that all shall rise from the dead and stand before God, and be judged according to their works." (Book of Mormon, Alma 11:40–41.) Eternal life is endless life, but it is also life with and like God. It is God's life. It is the highest form of salvation.

ALL MAY BE SAVED

Latter-day Saints believe that all men and women have the capacity to be saved. "We believe," Joseph Smith wrote in 1842, "that through the Atonement of Christ, all mankind may be saved, by obedience to the laws and ordinances of the Gospel." (Pearl of Great Price, Articles of Faith 1:3.) Stated another way, no one who comes to earth is outside the reach of Christ's power to save, no soul beyond the pale of mercy and grace. "God is no respecter of persons, but in every nation he that feareth him, and worketh righteousness, is accepted with him." (Acts 10:34–35.) Latter-day Saints do not believe in predestination. They do not believe that men and women are chosen or elected unconditionally to salvation or reprobation.

In Joseph Smith's day the great debate was between the Presbyterians and the Methodists. The Presbyterians subscribed to the tenets of Calvinism. They believed in such principles as the unconditional election of individuals to eternal life, limited atonement (only the elect are saved through Christ's atonement), the irresistibility of grace (no one chosen for salvation can resist the call to the same), and the perseverance of saints (one cannot fall from grace). The Methodists believed that men and women had a say in whether or not they would be saved, that there was a method, a system by which people could develop spiritually, that our works and labors in this life were necessary. They believed that a person could be in God's grace today and fall from it tomorrow, repent and be restored to that grace thereafter, and so on. For Joseph the Prophet, the two positions were extreme; truth took a road between them both.[5] Early on in his life, Joseph seemed to oppose the doctrine of predestination; this may explain why he seemed somewhat partial to the Methodists.

In regard to the individual responsibility men and women have to accept the doctrine of Christ, Latter-day Saints believe that the highest rewards hereafter and the greatest happiness

---

[5] See *Teachings*, pp. 338–39.

here are reserved for those who come unto Christ and accept his gospel. Though they acknowledge the decency of men and women of goodwill everywhere, the effort of many outside the Christian faith to make a positive difference in the world, and the nobility and refined character of so many who adopt other religious views, still the Latter-day Saints hold to the position that Jesus is the Christ, the Messiah, the Savior of all men and women. His message and redemptive labors are infinite in scope and meant to be accepted by all. He will one day return in glory to the earth, assume responsibility for the purification of this planet, and reign as King of kings and Lord of lords.

CHAPTER 5

THE ORIGIN AND DESTINY OF MAN

Three questions have haunted men and women from the beginning of time: Where did I come from? Why am I here? Where am I going? All three questions deal with meaning, with purpose in life. How we choose to answer or ignore them will determine largely how we live our lives. Latter-day Saints do not claim to have all the answers to life's puzzles, but they do claim to have some. This chapter will focus on the LDS view of life before, life now, and life hereafter.

THE LIFE BEFORE

From a Latter-day Saint perspective, we did not suddenly spring into existence at the time of our mortal birth. We have always lived. Others outside the LDS faith have sensed there is more to life than living and dying, more to what we do here than meets the physical eye. Many have perceived that this stage of our journey is but a part of a larger drama. William Wordsworth penned the following:

> Our birth is but a sleep and a forgetting:
> The Soul that rises with us, our life's Star,
> Hath had elsewhere its setting,

And cometh from afar:
Not in entire forgetfulness,
And not in utter nakedness,
But trailing clouds of glory do we come
From God, who is our home:
Heaven lies about us in our infancy![1]

Marcel Proust, the influential French novelist, wrote, "Everything in our life happens as though we entered upon it with a load of obligations contracted in a previous existence . . . obligations whose sanction is not of this present life, [that] seem to belong to a different world, founded on kindness, scruples, sacrifice, a world entirely different from this one, a world whence we emerge to be born on this earth, before returning thither."[2]

Latter-day Saints believe that men and women are literally the spirit sons and daughters of God, that we lived in a premortal existence before birth, that we grew and progressed in that "first estate," all in preparation for this "second estate." In that world men and women were separate and distinct spirit personages, and they had consciousness, volition, gender, and moral agency. They developed and matured according to their adherence to God's eternal law, and in spite of the fact that they walked and talked with God, it was necessary for them to exercise faith in God's plan for the ultimate salvation of his children. The Latter-day Saints believe that God is literally the Father of our spirits (Numbers 16:22), that we inherit from him divine capacities, the seeds of godliness.

In 1909, the Church's First Presidency wrote, "The Church of Jesus Christ of Latter-day Saints, basing its belief on divine revelation, ancient and modern, proclaims man to be the direct and lineal offspring of Deity. . . . By His almighty power He organized the earth, and all that it contains, from spirit and element, which exist co-eternally with Himself. . . .

---

[1] "Ode: Intimations of Immortality from Recollections of Early Childhood," *English Romantic Poetry and Prose,* ed. Alfred Noyes (New York: Oxford University Press, 1956), pp. 327–28.
[2] In Gabriel Marcel, *Homo Viator* (New York: Harper & Row, 1963), p. 8.

Man is the child of God, formed in the divine image and endowed with divine attributes." Further, they said:

> The doctrine of the pre-existence—revealed so plainly, particularly in latter days, pours a wonderful flood of light upon the otherwise mysterious problem of man's origin. It shows that *man, as a spirit, was begotten and born of heavenly parents, and reared to maturity in the eternal mansions of the Father, prior to coming upon the earth in a temporal body to undergo an experience in mortality. It teaches that all men existed in the spirit before any man existed in the flesh,* and that all who have inhabited the earth since Adam have taken bodies and become souls in like manner.[3]

In the long expanse of time before we were born into mortality, the spirit sons and daughters of God developed talents, strengths, and capacities. In a sense, no two people remained alike. Latter-day Saints teach that the greatest in the family of God was Jehovah, who eventually took a body and became Jesus of Nazareth, the Redeemer of mankind. Jehovah was the firstborn of the Father, meaning the firstborn spirit child, the heir, the one entitled to the birthright of God. In this sense, the Latter-day Saints speak of Jehovah or Jesus Christ as their "elder brother" in the premortal spirit world. Jehovah was the advocate for the Father's plan of salvation, the one who volunteered in that premortal existence to put into effect the terms and conditions of that divine plan and, more specifically, to suffer and die as Savior. Another spirit child of God offered to save mankind by an alternative plan. Lucifer stepped forward and said, "Behold, here am I, send me, I will be thy son, and I will redeem all mankind, that one soul shall not be lost, and surely I will do it; wherefore give me thine honor."[4] God later explained to Moses:

---

[3] From "The Origin of Man," November 1909, in *Messages of the First Presidency* 4:199–206; emphasis added.
[4] Pearl of Great Price, Moses 4:1.

But, behold, my Beloved Son, which was my Beloved and Chosen from the beginning, said unto me—Father, thy will be done, and the glory be thine forever.

Wherefore, because that Satan rebelled against me, and sought to destroy the agency of man, which I, the Lord God, had given him, and also, that I should give unto him mine own power; by the power of mine Only Begotten, I caused that he should be cast down;

And he became Satan, yea, even the devil, the father of all lies, to deceive and to blind men, and to lead them captive at his will, even as many as would not hearken unto my voice. (Pearl of Great Price, Moses 4:2–4.)

"The contention in heaven was," Joseph Smith explained, "Jesus said there would be certain souls that would not be saved; and the devil said he could save them all, and laid his plans before the grand council, who gave their vote in favor of Jesus Christ. So the devil rose up in rebellion against God, and was cast down, with all who put up their heads for him."[5] The Latter-day Saints believe that the fall of Lucifer and his followers—one third of the spirit children of the Father (Revelation 12:4; D&C 29:36), allusions to which are found in the Bible (Isaiah 14:12–15; Luke 10:18; Revelation 12:7–9)—signaled the perpetuation of evil on earth. Lucifer, or Satan, with his minions, became the enemy of God and of all righteousness and to this day seeks to destroy the souls of men and women.

Truth was taught in that premortal sphere. The gospel was declared. The sons and daughters of God came to understand and appreciate the goodness and powers of Deity. They recognized that God the Father, the Supreme Being, was possessed of a physical, resurrected, immortal, and glorified body. They came to know that the fullness of eternal joy was to be had through becoming as God is; through coming to earth, taking a physical body, growing and maturing in their ability to overcome temptations and deal with the stresses of this world; and through qualifying, by accepting the gospel of

---

[5] *Teachings,* p. 357.

Jesus Christ and incorporating the Lord's divine nature into their own, to return to the presence of God as living souls, spirits and bodies having been inseparably joined through the resurrection, never again to be divided.

Before coming to earth, the sons and daughters of God were told that as mortals they would be required to walk by faith, to operate in this second estate without full knowledge of what they did and who they were in the life before. A veil of forgetfulness would be placed over their minds. One early Church leader suggested what might have been said before we left: "Remember you go [to earth] on this condition, that is, you are to forget all things you ever saw, or knew to be transacted in the spirit world; . . . you must go and become one of the most helpless of all beings that I have created, while in your infancy, subject to sickness, pain, tears, mourning, sorrow and death. But *when truth shall touch the cords of your heart they will vibrate; then intelligence shall illuminate your mind, and shed its lustre in your soul, and you shall begin to understand the things you once knew,* but which had gone from you; you shall then begin to understand and know the object of your creation."[6]

MORTAL LIFE

Mortality constitutes the second phase of our eternal existence. As we have observed, in this life we are to learn to walk by faith, to come to know the will of God—his purposes, his plan, his promises—through attuning ourselves to the quiet voice of conscience within us and by attending to eternal truths. Life is obviously a complex and in many ways incomprehensible experience, but to simplify, let me suggest that Latter-day Saints speak of two main purposes of mortality—to gain a physical body and to have experience.

As we mentioned in chapter 3, the Latter-day Saint view of the physical body is unusually optimistic in the Christian

---

[6] John Taylor, in "The Mormon," August 29, 1857, New York City; in *The Vision,* comp. N. B. Lundwall (Salt Lake City: Bookcraft, n.d.), pp. 146–47; emphasis added.

world. The body is corrupt in the sense that it is decaying and dying. The flesh is the means by which a fallen nature comes into being and thus the means by which sin and sorrow emerge. But the body is also the tabernacle of the human spirit and is, in conjunction with that spirit, a vital part of the living soul that will rise in the resurrection. Satan and his followers do not have a body. They are spirits; their consuming desire to possess a body is manifest in the New Testament account of the devils entering the Gadarene swine. (See Mark 5:1–13; Luke 8:26–33.) Joseph Smith taught, "We came to this earth that we might have a body and present it pure before God in the celestial kingdom [the highest heaven]. The great principle of happiness consists in having a body. The devil has no body, and herein is his punishment. . . . All beings who have bodies have power over those who have not."[7] Also, "Salvation is nothing more nor less than to triumph over all our enemies and put them under our feet. . . . No person can have this salvation except through a tabernacle,"[8] meaning, of course, a physical body.

Evidently some types of experiential learning take place with the physical body that could not be had in the premortal spirit world. Men and women in that sphere were certainly capable of such emotions as love and tenderness and compassion—as well as envy, jealousy, rage, and even hate, as illustrated in Lucifer's rebellion, his orchestration of what has come to be known as the "war in heaven." Yet the feelings and challenges associated with such things as physical desire, lust, hunger, thirst, and fatigue seem perhaps more suited to the physical realm. Latter-day Saints believe that one of the major purposes of mortality is to learn to overcome, to put things into perspective, to keep our passions and desires within the bounds the Lord has set. In regard to one particular phase of the physical body, the sexual desire, a modern apostle has written, "The mortal body is the instrument of our mind and the foundation of our character. The sacred power

---

[7] *Teachings,* p. 181; see also p. 190.
[8] Ibid., p. 297.

of procreation gives us an essential part in the plan. There are laws, eternal laws, set to govern our use of it. It is to operate in very narrow limits."[9] Some of the greatest challenges to faith come in the form of pain, abuse, seemingly meaningless suffering, ironic tragedy, and man's inhumanity to man. It is a tenet of the LDS faith that pain and suffering are an essential part of the plan—not something we seek out, to be sure, but a vital dimension of mortality. In the midst of enormous suffering in a miserable jail in Missouri, Joseph Smith wrote by way of inquiry, "O God, where art thou? And where is the pavilion that covereth thy hiding place? How long shall thy hand be stayed, and thine eye, yea thy pure eye, behold from the eternal heavens the wrongs of thy people and of thy servants, and thine ear be penetrated with their cries? Yea, O Lord, how long shall they suffer these wrongs and unlawful oppressions, before thine heart shall be softened toward them, and thy bowels be moved with compassion toward them?" Within moments he wrote the divine reply: "My son, peace be unto thy soul; thine adversity and thine afflictions shall be but a small moment; and then, if thou endure it well, God shall exalt thee on high; thou shalt triumph over all thy foes." And then later, to put all of Joseph's and the Saints' sufferings in perspective, the word came: "Know thou, my son, that *all these things shall give thee experience, and shall be for thy good.* The Son of Man hath descended below them all. Art thou greater than he? Therefore, hold on thy way, and . . . fear not what man can do, for God shall be with you forever and ever." (D&C 121:1–3, 7–8; 122:7–9; emphasis added.)

Latter-day Saints believe that God is all-powerful, that he *could* prevent all suffering, stop all abuse, remove even the possibility of inhumanity, and erase all pain—but he will not. The war in heaven was fought over moral agency, and the price to be paid by abuse of agency on the part of some is not as great as the price that would naturally entail from surrendering agency and thereby aligning ourselves with Lucifer's

---

[9] Boyd K. Packer, *Our Father's Plan* (Salt Lake City: Deseret Book Co., 1984), pp. 24, 26.

nefarious plan. Further, Latter-day Saints are encouraged to view death with perspective, not with finality. As we will note later in this chapter, death is merely another phase of life. To die is not to cease to exist but to be transferred to another field of labor. "Those that live shall inherit the earth, and those that die shall rest from all their labors, and their works shall follow them." (D&C 59:2; compare Revelation 14:13.) In what may be one of the most important addresses on the place of human suffering in the development of an eternal character, Spencer W. Kimball said:

> If we looked at mortality as the whole of existence, then pain, sorrow, failure, and short life would be calamity. But if we look upon life as an eternal thing stretching far into the premortal past and on into the eternal post-death future, then all happenings may be put in proper perspective.
>
> Is there not wisdom in [God] giving us trials that we might rise above them, responsibilities that we might achieve, work to harden our muscles, sorrows to try our souls? Are we not exposed to temptations to test our strength, sickness that we might learn patience, death that we might be immortalized and glorified?
>
> If all the sick for whom we pray were healed, if all the righteous were protected and the wicked destroyed, the whole program of the Father would be annulled and the basic principle of the gospel, free agency, would be ended. No man would have to live by faith.
>
> If joy and peace and rewards were instantaneously given the doer of good, there could be no evil—all would do good but not because of the rightness of doing good. There would be no test of strength, no development of character, no growth of powers, no free agency, only satanic controls. . . .
>
> Being human, we would expel from our lives physical pain and mental anguish and assure ourselves of continual ease and comfort, but if we were to close the doors upon sorrow and distress, we might be excluding our greatest friends and benefactors. Suffering can make saints of people

as they learn patience, long-suffering, and self-mastery. The sufferings of our Savior were part of his education.[10]

I hasten to add that Latter-day Saints are not ascetic. They do not seek out persecution or glory in pain. Rather, they believe we all had in the first estate an understanding of the nature of the second estate, even the difficult and challenging times ahead. And we agreed to face it all, knowing it would be a crucial part of our spiritual development. "Life is an obstacle course," one LDS philosopher observed. "And sometimes it is a spook alley. But the before [the premortal existence] was a time of visioning the after [this life]. And some of our prayers [here in this life] are like the gamblers', 'Give me the money I made you promise not to give me if I asked for it.' What does a true friend do in such a case? God will honor our first request, to let us go through it; and He will provide you with . . . the way to make it bearable. More, to make it productive."[11]

THE LIFE BEYOND

Birth and death are inextricably intertwined. We are born to die and die to live. In a sense, mortal birth is tantamount to a death in premortality: we die as to things as they were in order to enter the realm of mortality. In so doing, we move from eternity into time. Second, in this fallen world we must crucify the old man of sin within us and rise to a newness of life through the cleansing power of Christ's blood. Finally, we must pass beyond this vale of tears to inherit a far greater and grander existence; it is in dying that we are born into immortality. In mortal death we leave the realm of time and return to eternity.

Life's starkest reality is death. Death is "a subject which strikes dread—even terror—into the hearts of most men. It is

---

[10] "Tragedy or Destiny?" in *Faith Precedes the Miracle* (Salt Lake City: Deseret Book Co., 1972), pp. 97–98.
[11] Truman G. Madsen, "Human Anguish and Divine Love," in *Four Essays on Love* (Provo: Communications Workshop, 1971), p. 59.

something we fear, of which we are sorely afraid, and from which most of us would flee if we could."[12] It is universal, one thing that every mortal shares with every other mortal, in spite of earthly status or accomplishments. Every man or woman is born, and every man or woman must die. All are born as helpless infants, and all are equally helpless in the face of death. Even among those who see by the lamp of understanding, death is frequently viewed with fear and trembling. Joseph Smith is reported to have taught that "if the people knew what was behind the veil, they would try by every means to commit suicide that they might get there, but the Lord in his wisdom had implanted the fear of death in every person that they might cling to life and thus accomplish the designs of their Creator."[13]

Latter-day Saints teach that the transition from time into eternity is immediate. As the physical self breathes its last breath, the spirit self passes through a thin veil separating this world from the next. The powers of intellect and the feelings of the heart reside within the spirit of man, and so consciousness, awareness, identity, affection, and receptivity to truth continue with us into the next world. Early leaders instructed the Saints that the postmortal spirit world was all about us, and that very often loved ones who have passed away "are not far from us, and know and understand our thoughts, feelings, and motions."[14] On the one hand, death is a great leveler: it breaks all the bands of poverty, infirmity, and worldly caste and station. On the other hand, death is a great separator, an occasion wherein a "partial judgment" of the spirit results in a designated area of residence.[15]

One Book of Mormon prophet explained that there are two major divisions within the postmortal spirit world. The first is called *paradise*, the abode of the faithful, those who sought the truth, lived the truth, and embodied the truth. It is

---

[12] Bruce R. McConkie, in Conference Report, October 1976, p. 157.

[13] *Diary of Charles L. Walker*, 2 vols., edited by A. Karl and Katherine Miles Larson (Logan, Utah: Utah State University Press, 1980), 1:595–96.

[14] *Teachings*, p. 326.

[15] See Joseph F. Smith, *Gospel Doctrine*, pp. 448–49.

"a state of rest, a state of peace, where they shall rest from all their troubles and from all care, and sorrow." (Book of Mormon, Alma 40:12.) Those things that burdened the obedient—the worldly cares and struggles, the vicissitudes of life—are shed with the physical body. Paradise is a place hereafter where the spirits of the faithful expand in wisdom and grow in understanding, where the spirit is free to think and act with a renewed capacity and with the vigor and enthusiasm that characterized one in his or her prime. Though a person does not rest per se from the work to do in the world of spirits, he or she is delivered from the cares and worries associated with a fallen world and a corrupt body.

The other division of the spirit world, according to LDS teachings, is variously called hell, outer darkness, or spirit prison. In this realm of the life beyond, those who were wicked in mortality come face to face with their waywardness and come to see things as they really are. For them it is a time of confrontation, of painful awareness, of humiliation and repentance. "The great misery of departed spirits," Joseph Smith declared, "in the world of spirits, where they go after death, is to know that they come short of the glory that others enjoy that they might have enjoyed themselves, and they are their own accusers."[16] On another occasion he said: "A man is his own tormenter and his own condemner. Hence the saying, They shall go into the lake that burns with fire and brimstone. The torment of disappointment in the mind of man is as exquisite as a lake burning with fire and brimstone. I say, so is the torment of man."[17] Here those who died without a knowledge of the gospel of Jesus Christ will have an opportunity to be taught by those who officiate in the spirit world. They are not required to accept the message of Christ, for moral agency continues. But the opportunity will be provided for every living soul to hear the glad tidings of salvation, either in this mortal world or in the world to come.

---

[16] *Teachings,* pp. 310–11.
[17] Ibid., p. 357.

Latter-day Saints believe that the resurrection began when Jesus rose from the tomb in the first century. The Bible teaches that "the graves were opened; and many bodies of the saints which slept arose, and came out of the graves after his resurrection, and went into the holy city, and appeared unto many." (Matthew 27:52–53.) The Book of Mormon records that many people in the Americas rose from the dead at the same time. (Helaman 14:25; 3 Nephi 23:9–10.) The resurrection will resume at the time of the second coming of Christ. (See 1 Thessalonians 4:13–17.) At that point, many in the spirit world, specifically the faithful ones, will be resurrected and become immortal beings. Eventually everyone, even those who lived in gross wickedness, will rise from the dead. Coupled with the resurrection is the judgment, the time spoken of by many of the prophets wherein all men and women will account to God for their lives. "I saw the dead," John wrote, "small and great, stand before God; and the books were opened: and another book was opened, which is the book of life: and the dead were judged out of those things which were written in the books, according to their works." (Revelation 20:12.)

"In my Father's house are many mansions," Jesus said at the Last Supper. (John 14:2.) As to the nature of life after resurrection and judgment, Joseph Smith taught that there was not simply a division of heaven or hell. "From sundry revelations which had been received," he noted, "it was apparent that many important points touching the salvation of man had been taken from the Bible, or lost before it was compiled. It appeared self-evident from what truths were left, that *if God rewarded every one according to the deeds done in the body, the term 'Heaven,' as intended for the Saints' eternal home, must include more kingdoms than one.*"[18] Joseph then described a vision in which he saw three main kingdoms of glory—the celestial, terrestrial, and telestial (see D&C 76; compare 1 Corinthians 15:40–42), likened respectively unto the glories of the sun, the moon, and the stars.

---

[18] Ibid., pp. 9–10; emphasis added.

As recorded in the Doctrine and Covenants, the celestial kingdom of glory is made up of those who receive the covenant gospel, participate in the necessary sacraments or ordinances, keep their covenants, and remain true and faithful to the end of their lives. These are they "who have received of [God the Father's] fulness, and of his glory. . . . Wherefore, all things are theirs, whether life or death, or things present, or things to come, all are theirs and they are Christ's, and Christ is God's. . . . These are they who shall have part in the first resurrection. These are they who shall come forth in the resurrection of the just. . . . These are they who are just men made perfect through Jesus the mediator of the new covenant, who wrought out this perfect atonement through the shedding of his own blood." (D&C 76:56, 59, 64–65, 69.)

The terrestrial kingdom of glory is made up of those who chose not to receive the testimony of Jesus in mortality but afterward received it; who are "honorable men of the earth, who were blinded by the craftiness of men. These are they who receive of [God's] glory, but not of his fulness. These are they who receive of the presence of the Son, but not of the fulness of the Father." In short, the terrestrial are those who "are not valiant in the testimony of Jesus." (D&C 76:75–77, 79.) The telestial kingdom of glory is made up of those who "received not the gospel, neither the testimony of Jesus, neither the prophets, neither the everlasting covenant." (D&C 76:101.) These are they who were in life murderers, liars, sorcerers, adulterers, whoremongers, and divisive influences. (See D&C 76:82, 99–101, 103; compare Revelation 21:8; 22:15.)

Joseph Smith's Vision of the Glories included another category of persons—those who are resurrected, judged, and accounted unworthy of a kingdom of glory. These are the "sons of perdition," those who blaspheme or sin against the Holy Ghost, "vessels of wrath" who deny and defy the faith after having gained a sure knowledge of the truth. These have received the Holy Spirit, have had the heavens opened, have known God, and then have willfully chosen to sin against him. They say the sun does not shine while they see it. They are an enemy to the faith. Their sin is unpardonable. These are cast into outer darkness forever. (D&C 76:31–39, 44–48.)[19]

The Latter-day Saints believe that one does not require all of the answers to life's puzzling questions in order to face the challenges ahead; he or she only needs to know there is a plan, that there is meaning and purpose to it all. When we know who we really are, we come to act accordingly. Boyd K. Packer, a twentieth-century apostle, wrote, "If we have come to know our Father's plan, we are never completely lost. We know something of how it was before our mortal birth. We know much of what lies beyond the horizon on either side, and which path will be safe for us to follow. With a knowledge of the plan comes also the determination to live the principles leading to eternal life."[20]

[19] See also Matthew 12:31–32; Hebrews 6:4–6; 10:26–29; *Teachings*, pp. 24, 357–58, 361.
[20] *Our Father's Plan*, p. 60.

CHAPTER 6

GRACE, WORKS, AND SALVATION

F ew things are more difficult to achieve than balance—balance in our perspective and in our approach to life. It seems so much easier to swing to one extreme or the other. So it is in regard to the role of men and women in the process of salvation. The religious world is divided sharply on the issue: Are we saved by the grace of God alone, without works or righteous deeds on our part? Or are we saved by virtue of our efforts to be righteous? Or is there some combination of the two, some balance between God's mercy and man's obedience that leads to eternal reward? In this chapter we will suggest an LDS approach to grace and works, an approach that seeks to highlight the centrality and absolute necessity of the merits and mercy of the Redeemer, while at the same time placing appropriate responsibility upon the disciple of Christ for living the good life.

THE GOSPEL COVENANT

Latter-day Saints view the plan of life and salvation as a covenant, a two-way promise between God and man. On his part, God has done for us what we could never do for ourselves. He created the earth and all things on its surface. He opened the door for Adam and Eve to partake of the forbidden fruit and introduce mortality, a time of testing but also a time of experience and opportunity. And, of course, he made available redemption from individual sins and renovation from a nature that is easily enticed by the world. The act of redemption is indeed the great act of love on the part of the Eternal Father: "For God so loved the world, that he gave his only begotten Son, that whosoever believeth in him should not perish, but have everlasting life." (John 3:16.)

Like his Father, Jesus Christ has done for us what we could never do for ourselves. He suffered and bled and died for us. He redeems us from sin. He offers to change our nature, to make us into new creatures, people bent on goodness. He rose from the dead and thereby opened the door for us to do the same thing at the appointed time. The gospel of Christ is "the power of God unto salvation." (Romans 1:16.) The new life in Christ is not merely a cosmetic change, not only an alteration in behavior. It is in fact a new creation. Ezra Taft Benson, thirteenth president of the LDS Church, remarked, "The Lord works from the inside out. The world works from the outside in. The world would take people out of the slums. Christ takes the slums out of people, and then they take themselves out of the slums. The world would mold men by changing their environment. Christ changes men, who then change their environment. The world would shape human behavior, but Christ can change human nature."[1] Only Christ, who possesses the powers of a God, can do such things.

The scriptures are consistent in their declaration that no unclean thing can enter into God's kingdom. In theory there are two ways by which men and women may inherit eternal life. The first is simply to live the law of God perfectly, to make no mistakes. To do so is to be justified—pronounced innocent, declared blameless—by works or by law. To say this another way, if we keep the commandments completely

---

[1] Conference Report, October 1985, p. 5.

(including receiving the sacraments or ordinances of salvation), never deviating from the strait and narrow path throughout our mortal lives, then we qualify for the blessings of the obedient. And yet we encounter on every side the terrible truth that all are unclean as a result of sin. (Romans 3:23.) All of us have broken at least one of the laws of God and therefore disqualify ourselves for justification by law. Moral perfection may be a possibility, but it is certainly not a probability. Jesus alone trod that path. "Therefore," Paul observed, "by the deeds of the law"—meaning the law of Moses, as well as any law of God—"there shall no flesh be justified in his sight." (Romans 3:20; compare Book of Mormon, 2 Nephi 2:5.)

The second way to be justified is by faith; it is for the sinner to be pronounced clean or innocent through trusting in and relying upon the merits of Him who answered the ends of the law. (Romans 10:4; compare Book of Mormon, 2 Nephi 2:6–7.) Jesus owed no personal debt to justice. Because we are guilty of transgression, if there had been no atonement of Christ, no amount of good deeds on our part, no nobility independent of divine intercession, could make up for the loss. Truly, "since man had fallen he could not merit anything of himself." (Book of Mormon, Alma 22:14.) Thus He who loved us first (1 John 4:10, 19) reaches out to the lost and fallen, to the disinherited, and proposes a marriage. The Infinite One joins with the finite, the Finished with the unfinished, the Whole with the partial, in short, the Perfect with the imperfect. Through covenant with Christ and thus union with the Bridegroom, we place ourselves in a condition to become fully formed, whole, finished—to become perfect in Christ. (See Book of Mormon, Moroni 10:32.)

The means by which the Savior justifies us is wondrous indeed. It entails what might be called "the great exchange." It is certainly true that Jesus seeks through his atoning sacrifice and through the medium of the Holy Spirit to *change* us, to transform us from fallen and helpless mortals into "new creatures in Christ." But there is more. Jesus offers to *exchange* with us. In his epistle to the Philippians, Paul speaks of his eagerness to forsake the allurements of the world in order to obtain the riches of Christ. "I count all things but loss," he said, "for the excellency of the knowledge of Christ Jesus my Lord: for whom I have suffered the loss of all things, and do count them but dung, that I may win Christ"—and now note this important addition—"and be found in him, *not having mine own righteousness, which is of the law, but that which is through the faith of Christ, the righteousness which is of God by faith.*" (Philippians 3:8–9; emphasis added.) Paul's point is vital: justification comes by faith, by trusting in *Christ's righteousness*, in His merits, mercy, and grace. (See Romans 10:1–4; compare Book of Mormon, 2 Nephi 2:3; Helaman 14:13; D&C 45:3–5.)

Latter-day Saints acknowledge that though our efforts to be righteous are necessary, they will forevermore be insufficient. Paul teaches a profound truth—that as we come unto Christ by the covenant of faith, our Lord's righteousness becomes our righteousness. He justifies us in the sense that he *imputes*—meaning, he reckons to our account—his goodness and takes our sin. This is the great exchange. To the Corinthians Paul explained that "God was in Christ, reconciling the world unto himself, not imputing their trespasses unto them. . . . For *he* [God the Father] *hath made him* [Christ the Son] *to be sin for us,* who knew no sin; *that we might be made the righteousness of God in him.*" (2 Corinthians 5:19, 21, emphasis added.) As Paul explained elsewhere, Christ "hath redeemed us from the curse of the law, being made a curse for us." (Galatians 3:13; compare Hebrews 2:9.) From one LDS scholar's perspective, then, being justified is not only a matter of "acquittal" from guilt and sin but also of "being regarded as righteous in a future divine judgment."[2] Those who enter the gospel covenant and thereafter seek to do their duty and endure to the end the Lord "hold[s] guiltless." (Book of Mormon, 3 Nephi 27:16; compare D&C 4:2.) It is not that they *are* guiltless in the sense of having never done wrong; rather, the Holy One removes their blame and imputes—accounts or

---

[2] Sidney B. Sperry, *Paul's Life and Letters* (Salt Lake City: Bookcraft, 1955), p. 176.

decrees to the repentant sinner, the one who comes unto Christ by covenant—His righteousness. "For as by one man's disobedience"—the fall of Adam—"many were made sinners, so by the obedience of one"—Jesus Christ—"shall many be made righteous." (Romans 5:19.)

No one of us, of ourselves or on our own, is qualified to go where Christ is or to inherit what he has. But when we accept him as Savior by covenant, he treats us as though we had arrived. "A comparison may be made by reference to a man on an escalator. We anticipate that he will reach a given floor if he stays on the escalator. So a person will eventually be justified, but may be regarded as being so now, if he retains a remission of sins and continually shows his faith in God."[3] What, then, is expected of us? Latter-day Saints believe that more is required than a verbal expression of faith, more than a confession with the lips that we have received Christ into our hearts. There is no question but that the power to save, to change, to renew is in Christ. There is no question but that only Christ can do this. But Latter-day Saints feel that men and women must, to refer to the analogy, stay on the escalator, that is, stay in covenant. People who come unto Christ must have faith in Jesus Christ, repent of their sins, be baptized for the remission of sins, receive the gift of the Holy Ghost, and endure faithfully to the end of their days.

It is not that the Latter-day Saints believe that each of us must become perfect in this life to be saved, at least not as most people think of becoming perfect. Rather, it is expected that after we sin we return quickly to the light through godly sorrow and repentance and thus not continue in sin. The scriptures call for us to become perfect "in Christ" in the sense of yielding ourselves to his will, becoming one with him through the Holy Spirit, and becoming whole, fully formed, and complete in him. Stephen Robinson, an LDS professor of religion at Brigham Young University, has written:

---

[3] Ibid., p. 176.

The only other way of being justified, of being declared not guilty before God [other than the hypothetical means of living perfectly and thus being justified by law], is to admit our own imperfections, admit we can't be perfect on our own or save ourselves by our own efforts, and have faith in Christ our Savior. We must accept his offer of help by entering into a completely new covenant in which his efforts are added to our own and make up for our deficiencies. This is called justification by faith in Christ.

In the new covenant of faith, perfect innocence is still required, but it is required of the team or partnership of Christ-and-me, rather than of me alone. Because Christ and I are one in the gospel covenant, God accepts our combined total worthiness, and together Christ and I are perfectly worthy. As a result, in Christ I am clean and worthy today. My individual perfect performance remains a long-term personal goal and will be the eventual outcome of the covenant relationship, but it is not a prerequisite to being justified in the short run by faith in Christ.[4]

SALVATION BY GRACE

The theological debate over whether we are saved by grace or by works has continued for centuries. In reality, it is a fruitless argument that generates more heat than light. It is, in the words of C. S. Lewis, "like asking which blade in a pair of scissors is most necessary."[5] Mormons have too often criticized those who stress salvation by grace alone, and they have too often been criticized for a type of works-righteousness.

What is required of us, then? We must receive the ordinances of salvation, the sacraments of the Church. We must strive to live a life befitting that of our Christian covenant. We must do all in our power to overcome sin, put off the natural man, and deny ourselves of all ungodliness. These things evidence our part of the gospel covenant. They allow us, in fact, to remain in the covenant with Christ, even as we occasion-

[4] *Believing Christ* (Salt Lake City: Deseret Book Co., 1992), pp. 43–44.
[5] *Mere Christianity*, p. 129.

ally stumble and fall short of the ideal. Latter-day Saint scripture attests that good works are necessary, but they are not sufficient. The harder questions are: In whom do I trust? On whom do I rely? Is my reliance on Christ's works, or do I strive to save myself?

The doctrine that we must rely on the grace of Christ is found throughout LDS scripture. One Book of Mormon prophet taught that since man had fallen, he could not merit anything of himself, but that deliverance from sin and death comes through the sufferings and death of Christ. (Alma 22:14.) Another called upon his people to exercise unshaken faith in the Redeemer, "*relying wholly* upon the merits of him who is mighty to save." (2 Nephi 31:19, emphasis added.) A later Book of Mormon leader beckoned to his people to be "watchful unto prayer, *relying alone* upon the merits of Christ, who was the author and the finisher of their faith." (Moroni 6:4, emphasis added.) Perhaps one of the best-known Book of Mormon passages in LDS circles is the following: "We labor diligently to write, to persuade our children, and also our brethren, to believe in Christ, and to be reconciled to God; for we know that it is by grace that we are saved, after all we can do." (2 Nephi 25:23; see also 10:24.) People are redeemed because of the righteousness of the Redeemer. (See Book of Mormon, 2 Nephi 2:3.) Finally, from the Doctrine and Covenants comes a touching invitation to believe in Christ, a reminder of the importance of the Master's merits: "Listen to him who is the advocate with the Father, who is pleading your cause before him—saying: Father, *behold the sufferings and death of him who did no sin,* in whom thou wast well pleased; *behold the blood of thy Son which was shed,* the blood of him whom thou gavest that thyself might be glorified; wherefore, Father, spare these my brethren that believe on my name, that they may come unto me and have everlasting life." (D&C 45:3–5, emphasis added.)

"How else could salvation possibly come?" Bruce R. McConkie, an LDS leader asked. "Can man save himself? Can he resurrect himself? Can he create a celestial kingdom and decree his own admission thereto? Salvation must and does originate with God, and if man is to receive it, God must bestow it upon him, which bestowal is a manifestation of grace. . . . Salvation does not come by the works and performances of the law of Moses, nor by 'circumcision,' nor by 'the law of commandments contained in ordinances' . . . , nor does it come by any good works standing alone. No matter how righteous a man might be, no matter how great and extensive his good works, he could not save himself. Salvation is in Christ and comes through his atonement."[6] Or as another Church leader, Dallin H. Oaks, observed, "Man unquestionably has impressive powers and can bring to pass great things by tireless efforts and indomitable will. But after all our obedience and good works, we cannot be saved from the effect of our sins without the grace extended by the atonement of Jesus Christ."[7]

To Latter-day Saints, the grace of Jesus Christ is not only a final spiritual boost that will allow us to move into heaven hereafter but also an enabling power, a divine dynamism that enables us to meet life's challenges in the here and now, to do things we could never do on our own. The Great Physician does more than heal the sin-sick soul. He ministers relief to the disconsolate, comfort to the bereaved, strength to those who have been battered and scarred by the ironies of this existence. "The Savior's victory," writes one author, "can compensate not only for our sins but also for our inadequacies; for our deliberate mistakes but also for our sins committed in ignorance, our errors of judgment, and our unavoidable imperfections. Our ultimate aspiration is more than being forgiven of sin—we seek to become holy, endowed affirmatively with Christlike attributes, at one with him, like him. Divine grace is the only source that can finally fulfill that aspiration, after all we can do."[8]

---

[6] *Doctrinal New Testament Commentary*, 3 vols. (Salt Lake City: Bookcraft, 1965–73), 2:499–500.

[7] Conference Report, October 1988, p. 78.

[8] Bruce C. Hafen, *The Broken Heart* (Salt Lake City: Deseret Book Co., 1989), p. 20.

THE DELICATE BALANCE

As we have seen already, the grace of God, manifest primarily in the gift of his Son Jesus Christ, is a necessary condition for salvation; there is no way, in time or eternity, that man could produce the plan of salvation, for such is the work of God. But, from an LDS perspective, the grace of God is a gift to humankind, a gift that must be perceived and received to be efficacious. The works of man—the ordinances or sacraments of salvation, the deeds of service and acts of Christian charity and mercy—are necessary for salvation; they evidence man's commitment and fulfill his covenant with Christ to do all in his power to live the life of a member of the body of Christ, or the church. But the works of man will never be enough to qualify one for the eternal prize; acting alone, without the grace and mercy and condescension of God, these deeds are but paltry offerings and are thus not sufficient for salvation. And thus it is that Moroni, the last prophet in the Book of Mormon, invites the reader to "come unto Christ, and be perfected in him, and deny yourselves of all ungodliness; and if ye shall deny yourselves of all ungodliness, and love God with all your might, mind, and strength *then is his grace sufficient for you,* that by his grace ye may be perfect in Christ." (Moroni 10:32, emphasis added.)

Few things would be more serious than encouraging lip service to God but discouraging or even downplaying wholehearted obedience and faithful discipleship. On the other hand, surely nothing could be more offensive to God than a belief that encourages the kind of smug self-assurance that comes from trusting in one's own works, relying upon one's own strength, and seeking to prosper through one's own genius. The Latter-day Saints teach that the key to understanding this sacred principle—the relationship between the grace of God and the works of man—is balance, balance and perspective provided through a careful search of the scriptures and a careful attention to the feelings of one's heart. One writer offered a parable that might prove helpful in understanding an LDS point of view on this vital matter:

A man is wandering in a hot and barren waste, and about to die of thirst, when he is caused to look up at the top of the hill where he sees a fountain of water in a restful setting of green grass and trees. His first impulse is to dismiss it as a mirage sent to torture his weary soul. But, being wracked with thirst and fatigue, and doomed to certain destruction anyway, he chooses to believe and pursue this last hope. As he drives his weary flesh to the top of the hill, he begins to see evidence of the reality of his hope; and, renewing his efforts, struggles on to the summit where he wets his partched lips, cools his fevered brow, and restores life to his body as he drinks deeply from the fountain. He is saved!

The author of the parable then offers these comments by way of interpretation:

What saved him? Was it the climb up the hill? Or was it the water? If he had remained at the foot of the hill either because of disbelief or lack of fortitude, his only means of salvation would have remained inaccessible. On the other hand, if he had climbed to the top and found he had labored in vain, he would have been worse off, if possible. . . .

The climb up the hill represents obedience to the gospel (faith in Christ, repentance, baptism of water, baptism of the Spirit, and endurance to the end); the water is that same eternal drink which Jesus offered the woman at the well. It is the atonement of Christ which is supplied as an act of grace.[9]

Latter-day Saints recognize the central, saving place of Jesus Christ. In response to William Ernest Henley's "Invictus," the haughty declaration that man is the master of his own fate and the captain of his soul, an LDS apostle, Orson F. Whitney, wrote:

---

[9] Glenn L. Pearson, *Know Your Religion* (Salt Lake City: Bookcraft, 1961), pp. 92–93.

Art thou in truth? Then what of him
Who bought thee with his blood?
Who plunged into devouring seas
And snatched thee from the flood?

Who bore for all our fallen race
What none but him could bear—
The God who died that man might live
And endless glory share?

Of what avail thy vaunted strength
Apart from his vast might?
Pray that his Light may pierce the gloom
That thou mayest see aright.

Men are as bubbles on the wave,
As leaves upon the tree.
Thou, captain of thy soul, forsooth!
Who gave that place to thee?

Free will is thine—free agency,
To wield for right or wrong;
But thou must answer unto him
To whom all souls belong.

Bend to the dust that head "unbowed,"
Small part of life's great whole!
And see in him, and him alone,
The Captain of thy soul.[10]

---

[10] *Improvement Era*, April 1926, p. 611.

CHAPTER 7

THE SACRAMENTS

OF THE CHURCH

Joseph Smith taught that when God chose to restore his everlasting gospel, it was fundamentally necessary to restore the priesthood or divine authority as well. In addition, the Latter-day Saints came to understand that the *sacraments* of the Church, what they call the *ordinances* of the gospel, were needed as channels of divine power, one of the means whereby men and women could partake of "the power of godliness." (D&C 84:21.) The Mormon prophet-leader consistently taught that the fundamental ordinances of salvation, like the gospel of Jesus Christ itself, have been in existence since the days of Adam and are forever the same.[1]

An ordinance is a law, a statute, a decree, a commandment, a requirement. "Among his laws and commandments, the Lord has provided certain *rites* and *ceremonies* which are called *ordinances*. These *ordinance-rites* might be pictured as a small circle within the larger circle of *ordinance-commandments*. Most of these rites and ceremonies . . . are essential to salvation and exaltation in the kingdom of God; some of them . . . are not ordinances of salvation, but are performed for the

---

[1] See *Teachings,* pp. 59–60, 168, 264, 308.

comfort, consolation, and encouragement of the saints."[2] In this chapter we will deal briefly with the ordinances or sacraments so fundamental to the faith.

ORDINANCES OF SALVATION

Latter-day Saints believe that the first principle of the gospel is *faith* in the Lord Jesus Christ. We have faith in Christ when we acknowledge him, not only as a great moral teacher but also as the Savior and Redeemer of all mankind, when we feel to trust in and rely upon his merits and mercy and grace. Once we come to know of him—of his majesty and greatness and holiness—it is but natural that we would begin to sense our own inadequacies and sins. And thus *repentance* is the second principle of the gospel. We repent when we literally "turn away" from our wrongdoings, when we confess and forsake them (D&C 58:42–43), when we come to have a new way of thinking and viewing the world. Forgiveness comes only from God through Jesus Christ.

Baptism. For Latter-day Saints, the first ordinance or sacrament of salvation is *baptism* by immersion. It is not optional; it is mandatory. It is an evidence of one's acceptance of the death and resurrection and atonement of Jesus. As the initiate is immersed completely beneath the baptismal waters, he or she participates symbolically in Christ's descent into the tomb of death and His rise to newness of life in the resurrection. "Know ye not," the Apostle Paul asked, "that so many of us as were baptized into Jesus Christ were baptized into his death? Therefore we are buried with him by baptism into death: that like as Christ was raised up from the dead by the glory of the Father, even so we also should walk in newness of life. For if we have been planted together in the likeness of his death, we shall be also in the likeness of his resurrection." (Romans 6:3–5.) Joseph Smith taught why baptism must be performed in a prescribed manner:

---

[2] Bruce R. McConkie, *Mormon Doctrine*, pp. 548–49; emphasis in original.

God has set many signs on the earth, as well as in the heavens; for instance, the oak of the forest, the fruit of the tree, the herb of the field, all bear a sign that seed hath been planted there; for it is a decree of the Lord that every tree, plant, and herb bearing seed should bring forth of its kind, and cannot come forth after any other law or principle. Upon the same principle do I contend that baptism is a sign ordained of God, for the believer in Christ to take upon himself in order to enter into the kingdom of God. . . . Those who seek to enter in any other way will seek in vain; for God will not receive them, neither will the angels acknowledge their works as accepted, for they have not obeyed the ordinances, nor attended to the signs which God ordained for the salvation of man, to prepare him for, and give him a title to, a celestial glory. . . .

Baptism is a sign to God, to angels, and to heaven that we do the will of God, and there is no other way beneath the heavens whereby God hath ordained for man to come to him to be saved, and enter into the Kingdom of God, except faith in Jesus Christ, repentance, and baptism for the remission of sins, and any other course is in vain.[3]

Water baptism satisfies the first half of the Savior's commission to be born of water and of the Spirit. (John 3:5.) Though the Latter-day Saints speak often of having their sins "washed away" in the waters of baptism (compare Acts 22:16; D&C 39:10), in fact the actual cleansing of sins does not take place until they are confirmed members of the Church and receive the Holy Spirit (see Book of Mormon, 2 Nephi 31:17; Moroni 6:4).

The covenant with Christ at the time of baptism entails more than individual worthiness and a life of personal purity, more than a vertical obligation. The Saint's horizontal obligation, his obligation to his fellow mortals, is enunciated (along with his obligation to God) by a Book of Mormon prophet as follows: "As ye are desirous to come into the fold of God, and to be called his people, and are willing to bear one another's

---

[3] *Teachings*, p. 198.

burdens, that they may be light; yea, and are willing to mourn with those that mourn; yea, and comfort those that stand in need of comfort, and to stand as witnesses of God at all times and in all things, and in all places that ye may be in, even until death, that ye may be redeemed of God, and be numbered with those of the first resurrection, that ye may have eternal life—now I say unto you, if this be the desire of your hearts, what have you against being baptized in the name of the Lord, as a witness before him that ye have entered into a covenant with him, that ye will serve him and keep his commandments, that he may pour out his Spirit more abundantly upon you?" (Mosiah 18:8–10.)

Laying on of Hands for the Gift of the Holy Ghost. The next ordinance of salvation is confirmation, the laying on of hands, by those with proper authority (the Melchizedek Priesthood), for the reception of the Spirit. This also is not optional; it is mandatory. Latter-day Saints believe that one must have hands laid upon the head, be confirmed a member of The Church of Jesus Christ of Latter-day Saints, and be told, "Receive the Holy Ghost." The gift of the Holy Ghost is the right to the companionship of the Spirit, the third member of the Godhead, based upon personal worthiness. (See 1 Corinthians 3:16–17; 6:19–20.) Joseph Smith taught that one may receive promptings or impressions of the Spirit prior to baptism, but that the gift of the Holy Ghost or constant companionship is granted only after an authorized baptism. "There is a difference," he said, "between the Holy Ghost and the gift of the Holy Ghost. Cornelius [see Acts 10] received the Holy Ghost before he was baptized, which was the convincing power of God unto him of the truth of the gospel, but he could not receive the gift of the Holy Ghost until after he was baptized. Had he not taken this sign or ordinance upon him, the Holy Ghost which convinced him of the truth of God, would have left him."[4]

Jesus taught that all people must be born again, born from above, born of the Spirit. (John 3:3–5; see also Book of

---

[4] Ibid., p. 199.

Mormon, Mosiah 27:24–26.) Being born again comes as the Holy Spirit of God begins to quicken or make alive the spiritual capacity of men and women, as the candidate for salvation begins to put away "the old man of sin" and put on Christ. (Romans 6:6.) Baptism, standing alone, is insufficient to enable one to be born again. The Holy Ghost, who serves as a revelator and a sanctifier, has the power to burn filth and dross from the human soul as though by fire, thus giving rise to the phrase *baptism by fire*. Though that new birth may come in a dramatic, sudden encounter with the powers of godliness, Latter-day Saints believe that most men and women are born again gradually, steadily over time, as the Spirit begins to work a mighty change within them. Ezra Taft Benson, president of the Church in the late twentieth century, thus taught, "We must be cautious as we discuss . . . remarkable examples [of rebirth]. Though they are real and powerful, they are the exception more than the rule. For every [one of these], there are hundreds and thousands of people who find the process of repentance much more subtle, much more imperceptible. Day by day they move closer to the Lord, little realizing they are building a godlike life."[5]

For a large segment of the Christian world, being born again comes through receiving the sacraments of the church. For another large segment, being born again comes through a personal spiritual experience. Joseph Smith taught that truth takes a road between these two extremes—that "being born again comes by the Spirit of God through ordinances."[6] Finally, as to its necessity, he said, "Except a man be born again, he cannot see the kingdom of God. This eternal truth settles the question of all men's religion. A man may be saved, after the judgment, in the terrestrial kingdom, or in the telestial kingdom, but he can never see the celestial kingdom of God, without being born of water and the Spirit, . . . unless he becomes as a little child, and is taught by the Spirit of God."[7]

---

[5] *Ensign*, October 1989, p. 5.
[6] *Teachings*, p. 162.
[7] Ibid., p. 12.

Sacrament of the Lord's Supper. As an outgrowth of the Passover meal at the Last Supper, Jesus introduced what Christians have come to know as the Sacrament of the Lord's Supper, or Communion. Like other Christians, Latter-day Saints partake of the sacrament (they use bread and water) in remembrance of his suffering and death, and more specifically, of his broken body and spilt blood. The prayer offered upon the broken bread illustrates the nature of the covenant, of man's promises to God as well as God's promised blessing:

> O God, the Eternal Father, we ask thee in the name of thy Son, Jesus Christ, to bless and sanctify this bread to the souls of all those who partake of it, that they may eat in remembrance of the body of thy Son, and witness unto thee, O God, the Eternal Father, that they are willing to take upon them the name of thy Son, and always remember him and keep his commandments which he has given them; that they may always have his Spirit to be with them. Amen. (D&C 20:77.)

The sacrament is distributed during the sacrament meeting, the main worship service in the Church on the Sabbath, as well as on other special occasions. It is a solemn and sacred period of devotion, a time of reflection, introspection, and covenant. It is a time for men and women to examine their lives, consider their commitment to Christ, and renew their covenants with God made at the time of baptism. David O. McKay, ninth president of the Church, observed:

> There are three things fundamentally important associated with the administration of the sacrament. The first is self-discernment. It is introspection. . . .
> Secondly, there is a covenant made; a covenant even more than a promise. . . .
> Thirdly, there is another blessing, and that is a sense of close relationship with the Lord. There is an opportunity to commune with oneself and to commune with the Lord. We meet in the house that is dedicated to Him; we have turned it over to Him; we call it His house. Well, you may rest

assured that He will be there to inspire us if we come in proper attune to meet Him.[8]

Latter-day Saints teach that in the same way the ancient Israelites presented their offering to the Levitical priest so that through that sacrifice their sins might be remitted, men and women in our day who have been baptized and received the Holy Ghost may, through their own offering—a broken heart and a contrite spirit (see Psalms 51:17; Book of Mormon, 3 Nephi 9:20; D&C 59:8)—be forgiven, have sins remitted, and be at peace through partaking of the Sacrament of the Lord's Supper.

> How can we have spiritual hunger? Who is there among us that does not wound his spirit by word, thought, or deed, from Sabbath to Sabbath? We do things for which we are sorry, and desire to be forgiven, or we have erred against someone and given injury. If . . . there is a feeling in our souls that we would like to be forgiven, then the method to obtain forgiveness is not through rebaptism, it is not to make confession to man, but it is to repent of our sins, to go to those against whom we have sinned or transgressed and obtain their forgiveness, and then repair to the Sacrament table where, if we have sincerely repented and put ourselves in proper condition, we shall be forgiven, and spiritual healing will come to our souls. It will really enter into our being.[9]

Ordination to the Priesthood. As we will discuss in more detail in the next chapter, Latter-day Saints believe that the priesthood is the power to act in the name of God. The priesthood is essential to the operation of the Church and vital to the promulgation of the gospel itself. Men must be ordained to the priesthood in order to participate in the sacraments of the Church and, more especially, in the saving ordinances of the temple.

---

[8] Conference Report, April 1946, p. 112.

[9] Melvin J. Ballard, *Improvement Era,* October 1919, pp. 1,026–27.

THE ORDINANCES OF THE TEMPLE

Most of the official meetings of The Church of Jesus Christ of Latter-day Saints take place in church houses. These chapels are found throughout the earth and are erected whenever a group of Latter-day Saints in the area is in a position to operate the programs of the Church. Sermons, worship services, religious instruction and study, many Church sacraments, and social gatherings either take place in the chapel or are organized there. The chapel is thus an important locus of Church activity. But it does not house all that takes place in the Church, especially some of the most important work of the LDS faith. The most sacred and lasting of Church sacraments are administered and received in temples.

The temple is the house of the Lord. It is a place where Latter-day Saints go to participate in ordinances of the gospel that are administered nowhere else. Some of the ordinances or sacraments that take place in temples include:

1. *The endowment.* Latter-day Saints speak of going into the temple to receive "the endowment." An endowment is, of course, a gift, and in this case the endowment is a divine gift of instruction and covenant.

> The Temple Endowment, as administered in modern temples, comprises instruction relating to the significance and sequence of past dispensations, and the importance of the present as the greatest and grandest era in human history. This course of instruction includes a recital of the most prominent events of the creative period, the condition of our first parents in the Garden of Eden, their disobedience and consequent expulsion from that blissful abode, their condition in the lone and dreary world when doomed to live by labor and sweat, the plan of redemption by which the great transgression may be atoned, the period of the great apostasy, the restoration of the Gospel with all its ancient powers and privileges, the absolute and indispensable condition of personal purity and devotion to the right in present life, and a strict compliance with Gospel requirements. . . .

The ordinances of the endowment embody certain obligations on the part of the individual, such as covenant and promise to observe the law of strict virtue and chastity, to be charitable, benevolent, tolerant and pure; to devote both talent and material means to the spread of truth and the uplifting of the race; to maintain devotion to the cause of truth; and to seek in every way to contribute to the great preparation that the earth may be made ready to receive her King—the Lord Jesus Christ. With the taking of each covenant and the assuming of each obligation a promised blessing is pronounced, contingent upon the faithful observance of the conditions.

No jot, iota, or tittle of the temple rites is otherwise than uplifting and sanctifying. In every detail the endowment ceremony contributes to covenants of morality of life, consecration of person to high ideals, devotion to truth, patriotism to nation, and allegiance to God. The blessings of the House of the Lord are not restricted to a privileged class; every member of the Church may have admission to the temple with the right to participate in the ordinances thereof, if he comes duly accredited as of worthy life and conduct.[10]

2. *Eternal marriage and sealings for the living.* Latter-day Saints believe and teach that when Christ gave the keys of the kingdom of God to Peter, James, and John, he gave them a power to perform ordinances that last not only until the end of this mortal existence but also throughout eternity. Jesus said, "I will give unto thee the keys of the kingdom of heaven: and whatsoever thou shalt bind on earth shall be bound in heaven: and whatsoever thou shalt loose on earth shall be loosed in heaven." (Matthew 16:19; see also 18:18.) Most civil marriages today, even those performed in a religious setting, contain the words "until death do you part." Marriages performed in LDS temples, by those given proper authority, contain the words "for time and for all eternity."

---

[10] James E. Talmage, *The House of the Lord* (Salt Lake City: Deseret Book Co., rev. ed., 1976), pp. 83–84.

Within the power to perform temple marriage (also called eternal marriage, celestial marriage, and the new and ever-lasting covenant of marriage) is the power to unite man and woman according to the laws of the land. But also within that power (the "sealing power"), Latter-day Saints affirm, is the right to seal that union through death and into the world to come. This sealing power also binds and seals children to their parents, thus making the parents and children an eternal family. Joseph Smith taught that in the celestial glory there are three heavens or degrees, and that in order to enter into the highest, one must participate in the new and everlasting covenant of marriage. (D&C 131:1–4.) "Except a man and his wife enter into an everlasting covenant and be married for eternity," he explained, "while in this probation, by the power and authority of the Holy Priesthood, they will cease to increase when they die; that is, they will not have any children after the resurrection."[11]

3. *Baptism and marriage/sealing for the dead.* Inasmuch as Jesus made it very clear that every man and woman must be born of water and of the Spirit (John 3:5), Latter-day Saints take very seriously the obligation to do missionary work throughout the world, in order that every person might be invited to come unto Christ in this manner. And what of those who have died? What of those who never heard Jesus preach? What of those in the first century who never had occasion to hear the testimony of Peter or Nathaniel or Paul? And what of those before or since that day, men and women throughout the earth, who have died ignorant of the gospel of Jesus Christ? Are they damned forever? Would God condemn them to hell because they did not come unto a Christ they did not know or accept laws or sacraments of which they were totally unaware?

Paul wrote to the Corinthians and sought to point up the inconsistency of believing in the atonement and redemption of Jesus Christ and yet doubting the truthfulness and reality of the resurrection: "Else what shall they do which are bap-

---

[11] *Teachings,* pp. 300–301.

tized for the dead, if the dead rise not at all? why are they then baptized for the dead?" (1 Corinthians 15:29.) That is to say (from an LDS perspective), "Why are you being baptized *on behalf of others* [The Revised English Bible, The New Revised Standard Version] if you do not believe in the resurrection?" Mormons believe that this New Testament passage alludes to a true practice of the first-century Christian Church, a practice wherein members of the Church were being baptized by proxy, in behalf of others who had died without proper Christian baptism.

Joseph Smith observed, "Aside from knowledge independent of the Bible, I would say that [baptism for the dead] was certainly practiced by the ancient churches; . . . The Saints have the privilege of being baptized for those of their relatives who are dead, whom they believe would have embraced the Gospel, if they had been privileged with hearing it, and who have received the Gospel in the spirit [world], through the instrumentality of those who have been commissioned to preach to them."[12] On another occasion he said, "If we can, by the authority of the Priesthood of the Son of God, baptize a man in the name of the Father, of the Son, and of the Holy Ghost, for the remission of sins, it is just as much our privilege to act as an agent, and be baptized for the remission of sins for and in behalf of our dead kindred, who have not heard the Gospel, or the fullness of it."[13]

This practice is closely tied to another doctrinal belief of the Latter-day Saints—that the gospel is preached in the postmortal spirit world. Latter-day Saints believe this is what Peter meant when he wrote, "Christ also hath once suffered for sins, the just for the unjust, that he might bring us to God, being put to death in the flesh, but quickened by the Spirit: by which also *he went and preached unto the spirits in prison.*" Further: "For *this cause was the gospel preached also to them that are dead,* that they might be judged according to men in the flesh, but live according to God in the spirit." (1 Peter 3:18–19; 4:6;

---

[12] Ibid., p. 179.
[13] Ibid., p. 201.

emphasis added.) In short, every person will have the opportunity, either in this life or the next, to receive the fullness of the gospel of Jesus Christ and enter into the everlasting covenant. As we noted in chapter 5, one dimension of the spirit world is sometimes designated as the "spirit prison," not necessarily because people who are there are in pain or agony, but because (1) they view the long absence of their spirits from their bodies as a bondage (D&C 45:17; 138:50), and (2) they are in the process of receiving and learning the truth, the receipt of which makes them free (John 8:31–32).

Between the time of Christ's death on the cross and his rise from the tomb, he went into the postmortal spirit world, preached his message, and organized the faithful, so that the message of truth might be available to all who are willing to receive it. (See D&C 138.) But the sacraments or ordinances of baptism, confirmation, ordination, and marriage/sealing are earthly ordinances and must be performed on this side of the veil of death. Thus the Latter-day Saints go into temples, receive the sacraments for themselves, and then return frequently to perform them in behalf of those who have died without them. "Every man," Joseph Smith pointed out, "that has been baptized and belongs to the kingdom has a right to be baptized for those who have gone before; and as soon as the law of the Gospel is obeyed here by their friends who act as proxy for them, the Lord has administrators there [in the spirit world] to set them free."[14] He also taught, "Jesus Christ became a ministering spirit (while His body was lying in the sepulchre) to the spirits in prison, to fulfill an important part of His mission, without which He could not have perfected His work, or entered into his rest. . . . It is no more incredible that God should *save* the dead, than that he should *raise* the dead."[15] And so Latter-day Saints are baptized, confirmed, endowed, married, and sealed by proxy for men and women who have gone on to the next world. In that sense, Mormons

---

[14] Ibid., p. 367.
[15] Ibid., p. 191.

feel the need to be anxiously engaged in the work of the ministry on both sides of the veil of death.

ORDINANCES OF COMFORT

Some of the other sacraments of the faith are, as noted earlier, for the comfort and consolation of the Saints and are not required for salvation. Some of these include:

1. *Blessing of babies.* "Then were there brought unto [Jesus] little children, that he should put his hands on them, and pray: and the disciples rebuked them. But Jesus said, Suffer little children, and forbid them not, to come unto me: for of such is the kingdom of heaven. And he laid his hands on them." (Matthew 19:13–15.) In an early revelation to the Church, instruction was given as follows: "Every member of the church of Christ having children is to bring them unto the elders before the church, who are to lay their hands upon them in the name of Jesus Christ, and bless them in his name." (D&C 20:70.) In harmony with that direction, worthy fathers who hold the Melchizedek Priesthood stand before the congregation and, in an act akin to prayer, bless their little children.

2. *Blessing of the sick.* The Bible records, "Is any sick among you? let him call for the elders of the church; and let them pray over him, anointing him with oil in the name of the Lord: and the prayer of faith shall save the sick, and the Lord shall raise him up." (James 5:14–15.) The disciples of Jesus "went out, and preached that men should repent. And they cast out many devils, and anointed with oil many that were sick, and healed them." (Mark 6:12–13.) The Lord commanded Joseph Smith, "The elders of the church, two or more, shall be called, and shall pray for and lay their hands upon [the sick] in my name." (D&C 42:44.) Holders of the Melchizedek Priesthood thus have the authority to anoint and bless the sick. By the power of the priesthood and through the faith of those involved (officiator as well as recipient of the blessing), healing miracles are wrought every day throughout the world.

3. *Blessings of comfort or instruction.* Latter-day Saints believe strongly in the power of God, as well as the divine power manifest through those who hold the priesthood. Members who are distraught, disturbed, or in special need of comfort, or who seek to better understand the will of God in their own lives, frequently turn to holders of the priesthood for special blessings. Fathers often lay hands upon their wives and children at a time of crisis, at a time when a child is starting school or going away to college, or on other occasions when the family member senses the need for help beyond personal prayers.

4. *Dedication of graves.* Latter-day Saints frequently hold a brief ceremony at the time of burial as a comfort to the bereaved, although this is not a required ordinance or sacrament. A holder of the Melchizedek Priesthood dedicates the gravesite as the final resting place of the deceased and prays that the plot of ground may be preserved against the elements until the time of the resurrection.

Ordinances or sacraments are a critical part of the LDS faith. Latter-day Saints believe they are one means by which the heavens are linked to the earth, by which the powers of God are accessed. Thus in a revelation recorded in the Doctrine and Covenants are found these words: "This greater [Melchizedek] priesthood administereth the gospel and holdeth the key of the mysteries of the kingdom, even the key of the knowledge of God. Therefore, *in the ordinances thereof, the power of godliness is manifest.* And without the ordinances thereof, and the authority of the priesthood, the power of godliness is not manifest unto men in the flesh." (D&C 84:19–21; emphasis added.)

CHAPTER 8

THE CHURCH
AND THE PRIESTHOOD

J oseph Smith gave instructions early on regarding the
establishment of a church. As we noted in chapter 1, on
April 6, 1830, the Church of Christ was formed, an organization that by the mid-1830s came to be known as the Church
of the Latter Day Saints, and by 1838 The Church of Jesus
Christ of Latter-day Saints. For the LDS prophet it was clear
that the reestablishment of the kingdom of God entailed more
than the reintroduction of saving truths or even of divine
powers and authorities. The restoration of the gospel included
the restoration of the "ancient order of things," both Old and
New Testament principles and practices, especially those of
the first-century Christian Church. He wrote in 1842, "We
believe in the same organization that existed in the Primitive
Church, namely, apostles, prophets, pastors, teachers, evangelists, and so forth." (Pearl of Great Price, Articles of Faith
1:6.)

THE MISSION OF THE CHURCH

Latter-day Saints believe that even though individuals are
responsible to receive the truth, love the truth, and live the

truth on their own, rich blessings come through working together with others. Joseph Smith explained that "the greatest temporal and spiritual blessings which always come from faithfulness and concerted effort, never attended individual exertion or enterprise."[1] The Church is the organized collection of believers, the body of Christ. Members of the Church are known as the Saints, the Latter-day Saints, to distinguish them from the Former-day Saints, believing Christians from earlier ages and dispensations of time.

The mission of the Church is to invite all men and women to come unto Christ. That overarching mission—to which all other doctrines are secondary and thus to which all Church programs and policies must be tied—is to be accomplished through three major endeavors:

1. *Proclaiming the gospel.* The proclamation of the message of the gospel (and for the Latter-day Saints, the *restored* gospel) is paramount. Joseph Smith taught that it is impossible to be saved in ignorance (D&C 131:6), and that "a man is saved no faster than he gets knowledge."[2] The Church of Jesus Christ of Latter-day Saints expends tremendous resources to see to it that members of the Church are educated, taught, and built up in the faith. In addition to three hours of direct instruction at church on Sundays, members are encouraged to undertake serious and daily personal study of the scriptures. Families in the Church are asked to study the gospel, enjoy social interactions, and counsel together about family projects and goals in a weekly "family home evening." Finally, LDS families are encouraged by Church leaders to conduct regular and consistent sessions of family scripture study.

The Church maintains a worldwide Church Educational System that has the primary responsibility for building gospel literacy and strengthening the faith and commitment of young people. Hundreds of thousands of LDS high school students are enrolled in seminary, a weekday religious education

---

[1] *Teachings*, p. 183.
[2] Ibid., p. 217.

program established in 1912. In seminary, students study the Old Testament for a full year, then New Testament for a year, followed in subsequent years by the Book of Mormon and the Doctrine and Covenants. College-age young people become involved in institutes of religion, programs of weekday religious instruction established in 1926, carried out adjacent to hundreds of colleges and universities throughout the world. Early in its history the Church established schools, colleges, and academies. Brigham Young University (Provo, Utah), the largest private, church-owned institution in the country, was established by Brigham Young in 1875. Since that time, the LDS Church has established Brigham Young University—Hawaii in Laie, a junior college (Ricks College in Rexburg, Idaho), LDS Business College (Salt Lake City), and a Church College in New Zealand. Though the thrust of the academic institutions is of necessity toward secular education, the schools are founded on religious principles, and students are expected to enroll for a designated number of religion courses as a part of a balanced curriculum.

Perhaps the proclamation of the gospel with which non–Latter-day Saints are most familiar is the Church's worldwide missionary program. All members of the LDS Church are asked to be missionaries, to look for occasions to share what they feel about God and Christ, about Joseph Smith and the Restoration, with family and friends not of the faith. In addition, young men and women, as well as older couples, devote themselves to voluntary, full-time missionary service for a period of time as an outgrowth of their desire to share their commitment about the faith with others.

2. *Perfecting the Saints.* The second avenue toward which people are invited to come unto Christ has to do with their development and spiritual maturity after their conversion and baptism into the Church. They are to be taught, built up, called to serve, and involved fully in the programs of the Church. One example of the kind of service in which men and women are involved throughout the world is what is known as home and visiting teaching. Home and visiting teachers are men and women who have the responsibility to

visit a designated number of families at least once a month, encourage the families to stay faithful, attend to concerns or problems, and discuss areas of success or difficulty with local Church leaders. Most members serve in this capacity.

The Church is financed by the tithes of its members, who are asked to pay one-tenth of their income to the Church. Tithing monies are used to build chapels and temples; finance missionary work; cover individual congregational costs for building maintenance and upkeep, as well as youth and social programs; and otherwise build the Church throughout the world. In addition, members are asked to participate in a monthly fast (to refrain from eating or drinking for two meals) and to contribute the cost of those meals or more to what is called a fast offering. Fast offerings are used to care for the poor, for those who may have had a financial setback, or for those who are temporarily out of work. These funds are administered by the local Church leader, the bishop or branch president. Those who have been assisted are asked, in an effort to maintain their dignity and self-reliance, to either repay the assistance or to work for a prescribed period of time on a Church project.

The family is the most important unit in time or eternity. The Church and its auxiliary organizations (for children, for youth, for men and women, and for single adults) exist to bless the lives of individuals and to help families in their quest for eternal life. The Church administers the gospel. That is, the Church is the vehicle, the organized structure, by which the plan of salvation is taught, the sacraments of the Church are administered, charitable service to others is orchestrated, and men and women come to develop a meaningful spiritual union with Jesus Christ.

3. *Redeeming the dead.* As we discussed in the last chapter, one of the major works of the Latter-day Saints takes place within temples. Mormons take seriously their responsibility to make available the ordinances (sacraments) of salvation for all, particularly for members of their own family. Their intense interest in family history and genealogical research is only partially because of their fascination with roots and fam-

ily trees. More specifically, members of The Church of Jesus
Christ of Latter-day Saints search out family records and complete pedigree charts for the purpose of identifying names of
deceased men and women for whom vicarious temple ordinances might then be performed. Men and women who are
in good standing in the Church, who have received the ordinances of the temple for themselves, then return regularly to
perform a vicarious act of service for those who have died
(who did not have the opportunity to receive the same for
themselves), and also to renew their own covenants and
remind themselves of their Christian obligations to God and
man. Latter-day Saints believe that vicarious work for the
dead is a sacred responsibility laid upon them, inasmuch as
"they [our kindred dead] without us should not be made perfect." (Hebrews 11:40.) Joseph Smith went so far as to say
that those Latter-day Saints who shirk this responsibility do
so at the peril of their own salvation.[3]

THE CHURCH AND PRIESTHOOD ORGANIZATION

Though the LDS Church does not have a paid ministry,
men who are called to positions of responsibility in the
Church are given authority to preside. That authority is the
priesthood. It is received by ordination, through the laying on
of hands of those with authority. (Pearl of Great Price, Articles
of Faith 1:5.) The priesthood is the power of God, delegated to
men on earth, to act in all things for the salvation of men and
women. It is divine authority, the authority Joseph Smith
stated that he received in 1829 from John the Baptist and
Peter, James, and John. In the Church, and on the local level,
worthy young men who reach the age of twelve have the
Aaronic Priesthood conferred upon them. Worthy young men
at the age of eighteen or nineteen have the higher or
Melchizedek Priesthood conferred upon them. As to the manner in which the work of the Church is carried on by a lay

[3] *Words of Joseph Smith*, p. 78.

clergy, Rex E. Lee, former U.S. Solicitor General and later president of Brigham Young University, has written:

> The dominant characteristic of almost all Church service is that nonprofessionals donate it. There is no such thing as a professional Mormon cleric who has trained for the ministry and then gone into it because he chose to do so. All ecclesiastical positions in the LDS Church, at all levels, are callings, and the calling comes to the individual, through inspiration, from someone else who has the authority and responsibility to make the calling. . . .
>
> As a consequence, the tens of thousands of positions, which include responsibilities for attending to the needs of the poor, comforting the widows, administering to the sick, conducting funerals, teaching the gospel, handling administrative and clerical details, serving members, conducting meetings, and counseling families are performed in the Mormon Church not by divinity school graduates, but by men and women age twelve and up who work at regular jobs for a living. . . .
>
> This does not mean, however, that trained professionals have no place in the Church. In cases where members work in administrative or teaching positions that replace secular jobs, those persons receive wages. For example, a well-developed administrative corps of paid staff employees handle the details of welfare, genealogy, missionary work, chapel construction, supply of manuals and other materials, the direction of the Church's educational system, and many other programs for the entire Church. Even locally, persons are hired to do such things as maintain the buildings and lands and administer some parts of the welfare and genealogy programs. . . .
>
> Sermons too are given by local members. The sacrament meetings (Sunday worship services) usually consist of one or two youth speakers who present three- to five-minute sermonettes, and one or two adult speakers, who deliver ten- to fifteen-minute talks. The sermons typically discuss scriptures, doctrine, and principles for living. . . .
>
> How can a church be run efficiently like this? How can it afford to entrust not only the organization, management,

and policy making to amateurs, but also the expounding of doctrinal principles? I have two answers to these questions. The first is pragmatic: the system works. The Church has been run this way since its organization in 1830. And quite well. The second is that the fundamental gospel principles of governance, cooperation, participation, and direction by the Spirit are plain and simple. They are principles that can be understood without the benefit of specific, college-level training, by the young and the old. They can be understood and taught today by people from all walks of life because they are the same principles that were understood and taught by carpenters and fishermen two thousand years ago.[4]

The Reformers sought to extricate themselves from what they believed to be a stifling priesthood hierarchy. In so doing, Protestant religious leaders began to refer to a "priesthood of all believers," men and women in the church whose sole authority was God and scripture. An early revelation to Joseph Smith declared that the gospel had been restored "that every man might speak in the name of God the Lord, even the Savior of the world." (D&C 1:20.) Each person, man, woman, or child, is entitled to pray, to come to God without human mediation, to know the will of the Almighty. Each person is entitled to feel divine promptings, become aware of what is the right and proper thing to do. And yet, Joseph Smith and his successors have explained, there must be order. The Mormon prophet thus observed that "it is contrary to the economy of God for any member of the Church, or any one, to receive instruction for those in authority, higher than themselves."[5] Further, he taught that "the Presidents or Presidency [the First Presidency, to be discussed shortly] are over the Church; and revelations of the mind and will of God to the Church, are to come through the Presidency. This is the order of heaven, and the power and privilege of this Priesthood. It is also the privilege of any officer in this Church to

---

[4] *What Do Mormons Believe?* (Salt Lake City: Deseret Book Co., 1992), pp. 74–76.
[5] *Teachings*, p. 21.

and policy making to amateurs, but also the expounding of doctrinal principles? I have two answers to these questions. The first is pragmatic: the system works. The Church has been run this way since its organization in 1830. And quite well. The second is that the fundamental gospel principles of governance, cooperation, participation, and direction by the Spirit are plain and simple. They are principles that can be understood without the benefit of specific, college-level training, by the young and the old. They can be understood and taught today by people from all walks of life because they are the same principles that were understood and taught by carpenters and fishermen two thousand years ago.[4]

The Reformers sought to extricate themselves from what they believed to be a stifling priesthood hierarchy. In so doing, Protestant religious leaders began to refer to a "priesthood of all believers," men and women in the church whose sole authority was God and scripture. An early revelation to Joseph Smith declared that the gospel had been restored "that every man might speak in the name of God the Lord, even the Savior of the world." (D&C 1:20.) Each person, man, woman, or child, is entitled to pray, to come to God without human mediation, to know the will of the Almighty. Each person is entitled to feel divine promptings, become aware of what is the right and proper thing to do. And yet, Joseph Smith and his successors have explained, there must be order. The Mormon prophet thus observed that "it is contrary to the economy of God for any member of the Church, or any one, to receive instruction for those in authority, higher than themselves."[5] Further, he taught that "the Presidents or Presidency [the First Presidency, to be discussed shortly] are over the Church; and revelations of the mind and will of God to the Church, are to come through the Presidency. This is the order of heaven, and the power and privilege of this Priesthood. It is also the privilege of any officer in this Church to

---

[4] *What Do Mormons Believe?* (Salt Lake City: Deseret Book Co., 1992), pp. 74–76.
[5] *Teachings*, p. 21.

clergy, Rex E. Lee, former U.S. Solicitor General and later president of Brigham Young University, has written:

The dominant characteristic of almost all Church service is that nonprofessionals donate it. There is no such thing as a professional Mormon cleric who has trained for the ministry and then gone into it because he chose to do so. All ecclesiastical positions in the LDS Church, at all levels, are callings, and the calling comes to the individual, through inspiration, from someone else who has the authority and responsibility to make the calling. . . .

As a consequence, the tens of thousands of positions, which include responsibilities for attending to the needs of the poor, comforting the widows, administering to the sick, conducting funerals, teaching the gospel, handling administrative and clerical details, serving members, conducting meetings, and counseling families are performed in the Mormon Church not by divinity school graduates, but by men and women age twelve and up who work at regular jobs for a living. . . .

This does not mean, however, that trained professionals have no place in the Church. In cases where members work in administrative or teaching positions that replace secular jobs, those persons receive wages. For example, a well-developed administrative corps of paid staff employees handle the details of welfare, genealogy, missionary work, chapel construction, supply of manuals and other materials, the direction of the Church's educational system, and many other programs for the entire Church. Even locally, persons are hired to do such things as maintain the buildings and lands and administer some parts of the welfare and genealogy programs. . . .

Sermons too are given by local members. The sacrament meetings (Sunday worship services) usually consist of one or two youth speakers who present three- to five-minute sermonettes, and one or two adult speakers, who deliver ten- to fifteen-minute talks. The sermons typically discuss scriptures, doctrine, and principles for living. . . .

How can a church be run efficiently like this? How can it afford to entrust not only the organization, management, obtain revelations, so far as relates to his particular calling and duty in the Church."[6]

At the general level, The Church of Jesus Christ of Latter-day Saints is presided over by a group of men known as the General Authorities. These men are headquartered in Salt Lake City, Utah, but in recent years some have assumed administrative responsibilities in different countries throughout the world. The president of the Church is acknowledged and upheld by the people as the presiding Prophet, Seer, and Revelator. He holds the same position in regard to the Church that Joseph Smith held. He has two counselors that officiate with him jointly; they constitute the First Presidency of the Church. Joseph Smith recorded the following in 1835: "Of the Melchizedek Priesthood, three Presiding High Priests, chosen by the body, appointed and ordained to that office, and upheld by the confidence, faith, and prayer of the church, form a quorum of the Presidency of the Church." (D&C 107:22.)

Working closely with the First Presidency are twelve men who form the Quorum of the Twelve Apostles. The counselors in the First Presidency and the Twelve Apostles are sustained by the Church membership as prophets, seers, and revelators. Latter-day Saints believe that the apostolic power held anciently by Peter, James, and John, and restored to Joseph Smith in 1829, is held by the First Presidency and the Twelve. "The twelve traveling councilors are called to be the Twelve Apostles, or special witnesses of the name of Christ in all the world." Further, this traveling council is called "to officiate in the name of the Lord, under the direction of the Presidency of the Church, agreeable to the institution of heaven; to build up the church, and regulate all the affairs of the same in all nations." (D&C 107:23, 33.)

Other General Authorities include the Seventy, priesthood ministers mentioned by Jesus in the New Testament (Luke 10), and the Presiding Bishopric. The Seventy have apostolic callings in the sense that they are called to be special

---

[6] Ibid., p. 111.

witnesses of the name of Christ in all the world and to build up the Church and regulate its affairs in all the world, under the direction of the Twelve Apostles. (D&C 107:25, 34.) The Presiding Bishopric are responsible for temporal affairs—for real estate, buildings and maintenance, welfare resources and projects, and so on. The First Presidency, the Twelve Apostles, and the Presiding Bishopric constitute the Council on the Disposition of Tithes, a group responsible for the expenditures of the Church. (D&C 120.) The General Authorities travel throughout the earth and are to be found in meetings and conferences of the Saints most every Sabbath.

THE DESTINY OF THE CHURCH

For Joseph Smith, the Church of Jesus Christ was also the organized kingdom of God on earth. As we have already noted, the Church is a service agency, an auxiliary to the priesthood in the blessing and benefiting of individuals and families. The Church deals in temporal matters, and it deals in spiritual matters. Latter-day Saints believe that all things are spiritual to God (D&C 29:34), that how we conduct our business and everyday affairs ought to reflect and bear witness of the spiritual realities within our souls. An LDS apostle has written, "A church and kingdom guided by the inspiration of heaven will always have whatever helps and governments are needed to save men temporally and spiritually. A religion that does not have power to save a man temporally and to care for all of his needs in this life certainly does not have power to save him spiritually and provide for all of his needs in the life to come."[7]

The Apostle Paul wrote to the early Christians concerning Christ's establishment of the Church: "He gave some, apostles; and some, prophets; and some, evangelists; and some, pastors and teachers; for the perfecting of the saints, for the work of the ministry, for the edifying of the body of Christ: till

---

[7] Bruce R. McConkie, *A New Witness for the Articles of Faith* (Salt Lake City: Deseret Book Co., 1985), p. 354.

we all come in the unity of the faith, and of the knowledge of the Son of God, unto a perfect man, unto the measure of the stature of the fulness of Christ." (Ephesians 4:11–13.) Because we are not yet perfect, because we are not yet united, and because all are in need of constant edification, the Latter-day Saints believe that the Church has performed and will continue to perform a vital function for the body of believers. Their leaders have taught that as the Saints become more united; as the individual members take more seriously their responsibility to serve and build others; as fathers and mothers devote themselves first and foremost to the preservation and development of the family, then eventually the Church will largely have fulfilled its role, and the Lord will make other provisions for his people. "The purpose of the church on earth is to prepare us for an inheritance in the church in heaven."[8]

---

[8] Ibid., p. 337.

QUEST FOR
THE CITY OF GOD

J oseph Smith boldly announced: "I calculate to be one of
the instruments of setting up the kingdom of [God envi-
sioned by] Daniel by the word of the Lord, and I intend to
lay a foundation that will revolutionize the whole world."
And how was this to be realized? "It will not be by sword or
gun that this kingdom will roll on," the Prophet said. "The
power of truth is such that all nations will be under the
necessity of obeying the gospel."[1] Joseph Smith's vision of
the kingdom of God was expansive. It consisted of more
than preaching and study and Sabbath services; it entailed
the entire renovation of the order of things on earth, the
transformation of man and the elevation of society. And at
the heart of that sublime scene was the doctrine of Zion, a
doctrine and a worldview that would shape the early
Church and point the Saints of the twentieth century
toward the eschatological ideal. In this chapter we will speak
broadly of the LDS idea and the ideal—Zion as a people or
community of believers, Zion as a specific place, and Zion as
a state of being—the pure in heart.

---

[1] *Teachings*, p. 366.

THE DISCOVERY OF ZION

Joseph Smith seems to have first encountered the concept of Zion (in a sense other than the holy mount or holy city in Jerusalem) in his translation of the Book of Mormon. The Book of Mormon prophets spoke of Zion as a holy commonwealth, a *society* of the Saints, *a way of life* that was to be established or brought forth under God's direction; those who fought against it were to incur God's displeasure. The municipals "labor for the welfare of Zion" rather than for money. In addition, in the words of the resurrected Savior, Zion was identified as a specific *place* in the land of America, a land of promise and inheritance for the descendants of Joseph of old. (Book of Mormon, 1 Nephi 13:37; 2 Nephi 10:11–13; 26:29–31; 28:20–24; 3 Nephi 16:16–18.)

A key moment in LDS Church history came during Joseph Smith's translation of the King James Bible. By December 1830, particulars concerning the patriarch Enoch and his ancient city of Zion were made known. A King James text of three verses on Enoch and his people was expanded to more than one hundred verses, uncovering knowledge of such things as the manner in which an entire society of antediluvians was spiritually awakened and stimulated to transcendent righteousness; the means by which this ancient people, formerly bent on selfishness and pride, had their souls changed, saw to the needs of the poor, and became "of one heart and one mind"; and how, through the application of such a divine philosophy, they were translated, taken from the earth into the bosom of God. (See Pearl of Great Price, Moses 7.) Enoch's Zion became the pattern, the scriptural prototype for the Latter-day Saints. In the months that followed, several revelations now in the Doctrine and Covenants spoke of the ancient Zion of Enoch and also provided the broad framework whereby the Latter-day Saints, through the principles of consecration and stewardship of properties, could lay the foundation for a modern society of Zion.

Consecration and stewardship was a means of establishing economic oneness among the Saints. Latter-day Saints were asked to consecrate all of their properties and holdings to God through the bishop of the Church. This they did by covenant. They then had deeded back to them a stewardship or inheritance, that portion of property or that assignment that they were to manage, expand upon, and be accountable for. Whenever the amount consecrated exceeded what was deeded back as stewardship, the residue or surplus went into the storehouse, the center of economic interests in the community. When the amount of resource generated by the stewardship exceeded the original agreed-upon stewardship, the excess or surplus also went into the storehouse. Surplus consecration and surplus production were used by the community to assist the poor, the widows, and dependent children. Many of the early Saints lived under this system in Ohio and Missouri, but by 1834 the specific implementation of this order of things was discontinued. Later versions of consecration and stewardship, sometimes known as the United Order or the Order of Enoch, were implemented in the Great Basin after the Latter-day Saints came West.

In some of the earliest revelations recorded was the repeated command, "Now, as you have asked, behold, I say unto you, keep my commandments, and seek to bring forth and establish the cause of Zion." (D&C 6:6; see also 11:6; 12:6; 14:6.) Zion thus came to be associated with the restored Church and the grander work of the Restoration, and the faithful could take heart in the midst of their troubles, for Zion was the city of God. (D&C 97:19.) Indeed, in speaking of the sacred spot where the people of God congregated, the Lord said, "Behold, the land of Zion—I, the Lord, hold it in mine own hands." (D&C 63:25.) Surely the King of Zion (Pearl of Great Price, Moses 7:53) would deal mercifully with his subjects.

ZION'S MULTIPLE MEANINGS

The idea that there was a specific location for the city of Zion within North and South America was made known by Joseph Smith very early. Some of the early Saints were called to preach among "the Lamanites" or Native Americans. Yet at that point in time, "it is not revealed, and no man knoweth where the city Zion shall be built, but it shall be given hereafter." They were told, however, that the location would "be on the borders by the Lamanites." (D&C 28:9.) It was on July 20, 1831, just as the leaders of the Saints had begun to arrive in Missouri, that the word came concerning the specific location of Zion. The Latter-day Saints were told that the land of Missouri was "the land which I [God] have appointed and consecrated for the gathering of the saints. Wherefore, this is the land of promise, and the place for the city of Zion. . . . The place which is now called Independence [Missouri] is the center place." (D&C 57:1–3.)

Zion is spoken of in scripture as a banner or *ensign* around which a weary or beleaguered people may rally. It is also a *standard* against which the substance and quality of all things are to be evaluated. The Saints were expected to judge all things by a set of guidelines obtained from a source beyond that of unenlightened man. Note the language of one of the revelations: "Behold, I, the Lord, have made my church in these last days like unto a judge sitting on a hill, or in a high place, to judge the nations. For it shall come to pass that the inhabitants of Zion shall judge all things pertaining to Zion." (D&C 64:37–38.) As an illustration of this principle, Joseph Young, brother of Brigham Young, explained that Joseph Smith the Prophet "recommended the Saints to cultivate as high a state of perfection in their musical harmonies as the standard of the faith which he had brought was superior to sectarian religion. To obtain this, he gave them to understand that the refinement of singing would depend upon the attainment of the Holy Spirit. . . . When these graces and refinements and all the kindred attractions are obtained that characterized the ancient Zion of Enoch, then the Zion of the last days will become beautiful, she will be hailed by the Saints from the four winds, who will gather to Zion with songs of everlasting joy."[2]

---

[2] Cited in "Vocal Music," in *History of the Organization of the Seventies* (Salt Lake City: Deseret Steam Printing Establishment, 1878), pp. 14–15.

In addition, Zion was to be the focus, the convergence, and the concentration of all that is good, all that is ennobling, all that is instructive and inspirational. In Zion all things are to be gathered together in one in Christ. (Ephesians 1:10.) In short, according to Brigham Young, "every accomplishment, every polished grace, every useful attainment in mathematics, music, in all science and art belong to the Saints."[3] The Saints "rapidly collect the intelligence that is bestowed upon the nations," Brigham said on another occasion, "for all this intelligence belongs to Zion."[4]

Zion is people, the people of God, those people who have come out of the world into the marvelous light of Christ. In this vein the early Saints were encouraged: "Let Zion rejoice, for this is Zion—THE PURE IN HEART; therefore, let Zion rejoice, while all the wicked shall mourn." (D&C 97:21.) Thus Zion is *a state of being,* a state of purity of heart that entitles one to be known as a member of the household of faith. Brigham Young therefore spoke of the Saints having Zion in their hearts: "Unless the people live before the Lord in the obedience of His commandments," he said, "they cannot have Zion within them." Further, "As to the spirit of Zion, it is in the hearts of the Saints, of those who love and serve the Lord with all their might, mind, and strength."[5] On another occasion Brigham affirmed, "Zion will be redeemed and built up, and the saints will rejoice. This is the land of Zion; and *who are Zion? The pure in heart are Zion; they have Zion within them.* Purify yourselves, sanctify the Lord God in your hearts, and have the Zion of God within you."[6] Finally, he asked, "*Where is Zion? Where the organization of the Church of God is. And may it dwell spiritually in every heart;* and may we so live as to always enjoy the Spirit of Zion."[7]

---

[3] *Journal of Discourses* 10:224.
[4] Ibid., 8:279.
[5] Ibid., 2:253.
[6] Ibid., 8:198; emphasis added.
[7] Ibid., 8:205; emphasis added.

ZION AS THE PLACE OF GATHERING

Isaiah the Prophet had spoken some seven hundred years before Christ of the "mountain of the Lord's house" being established in the tops of the mountains. (Isaiah 2:2.) In July 1840 Joseph Smith declared that "the land of Zion consists of all North and South America, but that *any place where the Saints gather is Zion.*"[8] The latter part of this statement—that Zion represented more than a place, a single location, but rather any locus of gathering—is significant. It broadens the notion of Zion to include areas around the world where the people of the covenant congregate. There was a larger vision of Zion manifest in some of the earliest revelations, especially in one recorded during a particularly difficult time of persecution in Missouri: "Zion shall not be moved out of her place, notwithstanding her children are scattered. They that remain, and are pure in heart, shall return, and come to their inheritances, they and their children, with songs of everlasting joy, to build up the waste places of Zion—and all these things that the prophets might be fulfilled. And, behold, there is none other place appointed than that which I have appointed; neither shall there be any other place appointed than that which I have appointed, for the work of the gathering of my saints—until the day cometh when there is found no more room for them; and then I have other places which I will appoint unto them, and *they shall be called stakes, for the curtains or the strength of Zion.*" (D&C 101:17–21; emphasis added.) The ward or branch is a local congregation. A *stake* is a geographical collection of wards, comparable in concept to the diocese in the Roman Catholic Church. In the dedicatory prayer of the Kirtland, Ohio Temple, Joseph the Prophet pleaded in behalf of the Saints, "that they may come forth to Zion, or *to her stakes, the places of thine appointment,* with songs of everlasting joy." (D&C 109:39; emphasis added.) The Saints came to understand that safety and refuge are to be found in the stakes of Zion: "Arise and shine forth, that thy light may

---

[8] *Words of Joseph Smith,* p. 415; emphasis added; spelling and punctuation corrected.

be a standard for the nations; and that the gathering together upon the land of Zion, *and upon her stakes,* may be for a defense, and a refuge from the storm, and from wrath when it shall be poured out without mixture upon the whole earth." (D&C 115:5–6; emphasis added.)

As to the center place of Zion, Bruce R. McConkie, a twentieth-century apostle, has written, "The center place! Let Israel gather to the stakes of Zion in all nations. Let every land be a Zion to those appointed to dwell there. Let the fulness of the gospel be for all the saints in all nations. Let no blessing be denied them. Let temples arise wherein the fulness of the ordinances of the Lord's house may be administered. *But still there is a center place, a place where the chief temple shall stand, a place to which the Lord shall come, a place whence the law shall go forth to govern all the earth in that day when the Second David* [Christ, the Millennial King] *reigns personally upon the earth. And that center place is what men now call Independence in Jackson County, Missouri,* but which in a day to come will be the Zion of our God and the City of Holiness of his people. The site is selected; the place is known; the decree has gone forth; and the promised destiny is assured."[9] And so, while the Latter-day Saints believe that Zion is a holy community, a gathering place for the Saints, a state of being, they also look to the day yet future when the center place of Zion will be built up and established, when the headquarters of The Church of Jesus Christ of Latter-day Saints will shift from Salt Lake City, Utah, to Independence, Missouri.

Although the Church will establish a significant presence in Independence, Missouri, and it will become a gathering place, the Center Place, yet there will always be, as suggested above, a need for the stakes of Zion throughout the earth far and wide, a need for the Saints to gather to their own lands and congregate with their own people. Spencer W. Kimball, twelfth president of the Church, explained, "The gathering of Israel consists of joining the true Church and . . . coming to a knowledge of the true God. . . . Any person, therefore, who

---

[9] *A New Witness for the Articles of Faith,* p. 595; emphasis added.

has accepted the restored gospel, and who now seeks to worship the Lord in his own tongue and with the Saints in the nations where he lives, has complied with the law of the gathering of Israel and is heir to all of the blessings promised the saints in these last days."[10] In addition, President Kimball taught, "The First Presidency and the Twelve see great wisdom in the multiple Zions, many gathering places where the Saints within their own culture and nation can act as a leaven in the building of the kingdom—a kingdom which seeks no earthly rewards or treasures. Sometimes, inadvertently, we have given artificial encouragement to individuals to leave their native land and culture and, too often, this has meant the loss of the leaven that is so badly needed, and the individuals involved have sometimes regretted their migrations."[11]

An Expanding Concept

Like the Church itself, the concept of Zion has grown and expanded as the Latter-day Saints feel they have perceived the plans and purposes of the Almighty. Erastus Snow, an early apostle, pointed out in 1884 that when the early Saints "first heard the fullness of the Gospel preached by the first Elders, and read the revelations given through the Prophet Joseph Smith, our ideas of Zion were very limited. But as our minds began to grow and expand, why we began to look upon Zion as a great people, and the Stakes of Zion as numerous. . . . We ceased to set bounds to Zion and her Stakes."[12] Likewise, Joseph Young explained that many Saints of the nineteenth century—moved upon by the spirit of prophecy and revelation, such that future events appeared close at hand—misconstrued and miscalculated on a number of matters, including the time when the Saints should return to Missouri and build up the center place of Zion. "The Holy Spirit brought many things close to their minds—they appeared

---

[10] *Teachings of Spencer W. Kimball,* edited by Edward L. Kimball (Salt Lake City: Bookcraft, 1982), p. 439.

[11] Ibid., p. 440.

[12] *Journal of Discourses* 25:30–31.

right by, and hence many were deceived. . . . I knew that faith and the Holy Ghost brought the designs of Providence close by, and by that means we were enabled to scan them, . . . but we had not knowledge enough to digest and fully comprehend those things."[13]

Zion is a place. Zion is a people. Zion is a holy state of being. In the words of Spencer W. Kimball, Zion is "the highest order of priesthood society."[14] It is the heritage of the Saints. "The building up of Zion," Joseph Smith taught, "is a cause that has interested the people of God in every age; it is a theme upon which prophets, priests and kings have dwelt with peculiar delight; they have looked forward with joyful anticipation to the day in which we live; and fired with heavenly and joyful anticipations they have sung and written and prophesied of this our day; but they died without the sight; we are the favored people that God has made choice of to bring about the Latter-day glory."[15] In that sense, as Joseph Smith stated, "We ought to have the building up of Zion as our greatest object."[16]

[13] Ibid., 9:230.
[14] Conference Report, October 1977, p. 125.
[15] Teachings, p. 231.
[16] Ibid., p. 160.

CHAPTER 10

THE HOUSE
OF ISRAEL

W. D. Davies once observed in an address at Brigham Young University that "Christianity has forgotten its Jewish roots":

> Mormonism arose in a place and time when many uto-pian, populist, socialistic ideas were in the air. It gave these a disciplined, organized American outlet and form: what it did was re-Judaize a Christianity that had been too much Hellenized. . . . Mormonism certainly injected and I hope will continue to inject, into the American scene the realism of Judaism and thus challenged a too-Hellenized Christian-ity to renew its contact with its roots in Israel.[1]

Indeed, the Latter-day Saints have a most unusual con-ceptual tie to ancient Israel and a serious engagement with the prophetic motif of the gathering of Israel. In this chapter we will examine the LDS views of the house of Israel, the gathering of Israel, and the manner in which the Latter-day

---

[1] "Israel, the Mormons, and the Land," in *Reflections on Mormonism*, ed. Truman G. Madsen (Provo: BYU Religious Studies Center, 1978), pp. 91–92.

Saints feel the ancient prophecies are to some degree being fulfilled through them.

A Chosen People

Joseph Smith's hold on ancient Israel and commitment to a "covenant theology" was strengthened in several ways. First, the Latter-day Saints placed great stock in the Old Testament and felt a kinship with its characters and events. Joseph Smith claimed that many of the ancient personalities—for example, Adam, Abraham, Moses—appeared to him and conferred priesthood authorities that they had held on earth. Second, the Saints' acceptance of the Book of Mormon further tied them to the people of Israel, inasmuch as the Book of Mormon is essentially a narrative and commentary upon God's dealings with another branch of the house of Israel. Third, Joseph Smith and his people saw themselves as Israel wandering toward a promised land, "in . . . the beginning of the rising up and the coming forth of [the] church out of the wilderness." (D&C 5:14; compare 33:5.)

Fourth, the Latter-day Saints came to believe they were of the actual physical lineage of Abraham, Isaac, and Jacob, literally modern "children of Israel." "The Mormons," noted Davies, "are a continuation of what the Fathers of the Christian Church were to come to call the Old Israel. But for the Mormons there is no Old Israel. They simply regard themselves as Israel in a new stage of its history."[2] Fifth, as children of Israel, the inhabitants of Zion were "covenant" people, participants in what they called the "new and everlasting covenant." Finally, the center of all religious activity was the temple. As with Israel of old, the ritual and religion of the holy temple gave broadened meaning to all that was undertaken in a city of holiness.

LDS theology attests that coming to earth through a chosen lineage or family is not accidental or coincidental, that one's actions and life in the premortal world affect how and

---

[2] Ibid., p. 81.

under what circumstances we enter mortality. Following our birth as spirits, being endowed with agency, each of the spirit sons and daughters of God developed and progressed according to their desires for truth and righteousness. "Being subject to law," Bruce R. McConkie has written,

> and having their agency, all the spirits of men, while yet in the Eternal Presence, developed aptitudes, talents, capacities, and abilities of every sort, kind, and degree. During the long expanse of life that then was, an infinite variety of talents and abilities came into being. As the ages rolled, no two spirits remained alike. . . . Abraham and Moses and all of the prophets sought and obtained the talent for spirituality. Mary and Eve were two of the greatest spirit daughters of the Father. *The whole house of Israel, known and segregated out from their fellows, was inclined toward spiritual things.*[3]

LDS doctrine attests that, like Christ (1 Peter 1:18–20) and Jeremiah (Jeremiah 1:5–6), many men and women were foreordained or foredesignated in that premortal world to specific assignments, callings, and blessings on earth. "Every man who has a calling to minister to the inhabitants of the world," Joseph Smith taught, "was ordained to that very purpose in the Grand Council of heaven before this world was."[4] Perhaps the greatest foreordination—based on premortal faithfulness—is foreordination to lineage and family: certain individuals come to earth through a designated channel, through a lineage that entitles them to remarkable blessings, but also a lineage that carries with it burdens and responsibilities. As a people, therefore, they enjoy what Brent L. Top calls "a type of collective foreordination—a selection of spirits to form an entire favored group or lineage." Yet, he adds, "although it is a collective foreordination it is nonetheless based on individual premortal faithfulness and spiritual

---

[3] *The Mortal Messiah: From Bethlehem to Calvary*, 4 vols. (Salt Lake City: Deseret Book Co., 1979–81), 1:23; emphasis added).
[4] *Teachings*, p. 365.

capacity."[5] In the words of Melvin J. Ballard, a twentieth-century apostle, Israel is "a group of souls tested, tried, and proven before they were born into the world. . . . Through this lineage were to come the true and tried souls that had demonstrated their righteousness in the spirit world before they came here."[6]

"Remember the days of old," Moses counseled his people, "consider the years of many generations: ask thy father, and he will shew thee: thy elders, and they will tell thee. When the most High divided to the nations their inheritance, when he separated the sons of Adam, he set the bounds of the people *according to the number of the children of Israel.* For the Lord's portion is his people; Jacob is the lot of his inheritance." (Deuteronomy 32:7–9; emphasis added.)

In speaking to the Athenians, the Apostle Paul declared: "God that made the world and all things therein, . . . hath made of one blood all nations of men for to dwell on all the face of the earth, and *hath determined the times before appointed, and the bounds of their habitation.*" (Acts 17:24, 26; emphasis added.) President Harold B. Lee explained:

> Those born to the lineage of Jacob, who was later to be called Israel, and his posterity, who were known as the children of Israel, were born into the most illustrious lineage of any of those who came upon the earth as mortal beings. All these rewards were seemingly promised, or foreordained, before the world was. Surely these matters must have been determined by the kind of lives we had lived in that premortal spirit world. Some may question these assumptions, but at the same time they will accept without any question the belief that each one of us will be judged when we leave this earth according to his or her deeds during our lives here in mortality. Isn't it just as reasonable to believe that what we have received here in this earth [life] was given to

---

[5] *The Life Before* (Salt Lake City: Bookcraft, 1988), p. 144.
[6] "The Three Degrees of Glory," in *Melvin J. Ballard: Crusader for Righteousness* (Salt Lake City: Bookcraft, 1966), pp. 218–19.

THE HOUSE OF ISRAEL

each of us according to the merits of our conduct before we came here?[7]

Who are we, then? President Lee answered:

> You are all the sons and daughters of God. Your spirits were created and lived as organized intelligences before the world was. You have been blessed to have a physical body because of your obedience to certain commandments in that premortal state. You are now born into a family to which you have come, into the nations through which you have come, as a reward for the kind of lives you lived before you came here and at a time in the world's history, as the Apostle Paul taught the men of Athens and as the Lord revealed to Moses, determined by the faithfulness of each of those who lived before this world was created.[8]

And yet the Latter-day Saints believe that coming to earth through a peculiar lineage involves much more than boasting of a blessing; it entails bearing a burden. "Once we know who we are," Russell M. Nelson said, "and the royal lineage of which we are a part, our actions and directions in life will be more appropriate to our inheritance."[9] Years ago a wise man wrote of the burdens of chosenness and of why it is that God had selected a particular people as his own. "A man will rise and demand," he suggested, "'By what right does God choose one race or people above another?'"

> I like that form of the question. It is much better than asking by what right God degrades one people beneath another, although that is implied. God's grading is always upward. If he raises up a nation, it is that other nations may be raised up through its ministry. If he exalts a great man, an apostle of liberty or science or faith, it is that He might raise a degraded people to a better condition. The divine

---

[7] Conference Report, October 1973, pp. 7–8.
[8] Ibid., p. 7.
[9] "Thanks for the Covenant," *1988–89 BYU Devotional Speeches of the Year* (Provo: BYU Publications, 1989), p. 59.

selection is not [alone] a prize, a compliment paid to the man or the race—it is a burden imposed. To appoint a chosen people is not a pandering to the racial vanity of a "superior people"; it is a yoke bound upon the necks of those who are chosen for a special service.

In short, God "hath made [Israel] great for what He is going to make [Israel] do."[10]

ISRAEL IN MORTALITY: THE SCATTERING AND GATHERING

As we pointed out in a previous chapter, those of Israel who follow the Light of Christ in this life will be led eventually to the higher light of the Holy Ghost and will come to know the Lord and come unto him. Latter-day Saints teach that in time those who follow this course come to know of their noble heritage and of the royal blood that flows within their veins. They come to earth with a predisposition to receive the truth, with an inner attraction to the message of the gospel. "My sheep hear my voice," the Master said, "and I know them, and they follow me." (John 10:27.) Those chosen to come to the earth through the favored lineage "are especially endowed at birth with spiritual talents. It is easier for them to believe the gospel than it is for the generality of mankind. Every living soul comes into this world with sufficient talent to believe and be saved, but the Lord's sheep, as a reward for their devotion when they dwelt in his presence, enjoy greater spiritual endowments than their fellows."[11] "The blood of Israel has flowed in the veins of the children of men," Wilford Woodruff, the fourth LDS president declared, "mixed among the Gentile nations, and when they have heard the sound of the Gospel of Christ it has been like vivid lightning to them; it has opened their understandings, enlarged their minds, and enabled them to see the things of

[10] W. J. Cameron, "Is There a Chosen People?" in James H. Anderson, *God's Covenant Race* (Salt Lake City: Deseret News Press, 1938), pp. 300–302.
[11] McConkie, *A New Witness for the Articles of Faith*, p. 34.

God. They have been born of the Spirit, and then they could behold the kingdom of God."[12]

And yet chosenness implies a succession of choices. Those who became Israel before the world was, those who were *called* in that pristine existence, must exercise wisdom and prudence and discernment in this life before they become truly *chosen* to enjoy certain privileges hereafter. LDS scriptures thus teach that "there are many called, but few are chosen." (D&C 121:34.) "This suggests," Harold B. Lee explained, "that even though we have our free agency here, there are many who were foreordained before the world was, to a greater state than they have prepared themselves for here. Even though they might have been among the noble and great, from among whom the Father declared he would make his chosen leaders, they may fail of that calling here in mortality."[13] And so the vivid reality is that lineage and ancestry alone do not qualify one for a divine family inheritance. To use Paul's language, "they are not all Israel, which are of Israel: neither, because they are the seed of Abraham, are they all children." (Romans 9:6–7.) In fact, as a Book of Mormon prophet reminded his readers, only those who receive the gospel and commit themselves by obedience and continued faithfulness to the Mediator of that covenant are really covenant people. "As many of the Gentiles as will repent are the covenant people of the Lord," he said, "and as many of the Jews as will not repent shall be cast off; for the Lord covenanteth with none save it be with them that repent and believe in his Son, who is the Holy One of Israel." (2 Nephi 30:2.)

Both the Old Testament and the Book of Mormon set forth in consistent detail the reasons why over the generations Israel has been scattered and how it is they are to be gathered. Speaking on behalf of Jehovah, Moses warned ancient Israel that if they should reject their God, they would be scattered among the nations, dispersed among the Gen-

---

[12] *Journal of Discourses* 15:11.
[13] Conference Report, October 1973, p. 7.

tiles. "If thou wilt not hearken unto the voice of the Lord thy God," he said, "to observe to do all his commandments and his statutes which I command thee this day [you will be] removed into all the kingdoms of the earth. . . . And ye shall be plucked from off the land whither thou goest to possess it. And the Lord shall scatter thee among all people, from the one end of the earth even unto the other; and there thou shalt serve other gods, which neither thou nor thy fathers have known." (Deuteronomy 28:15, 25, 63–64.) The Lord spoke in a similar vein through Jeremiah centuries later: "Because your fathers have forsaken me, saith the Lord, and have walked after other gods, and have served them, and have worshipped them, and have forsaken me, and have not kept my law; and ye have done worse than your fathers; . . . therefore will I cast you out of this land into a land that ye know not, . . . where I will not shew you favour." (Jeremiah 16:11–13.) The people of God became scattered—alienated from Jehovah and the ways of righteousness, lost as to their identity as covenant representatives, and displaced from the lands set aside for their inheritance—because they forsook the God of Abraham, Isaac, and Jacob and partook of the worship and ways of unholy men.

Though Israel is generally scattered because of her apostasy, the Latter-day Saints also believe that the Lord scatters certain branches of his chosen people throughout the earth in order to accomplish his purposes—to spread the blood and influence of Abraham throughout the globe. (See Book of Mormon, 1 Nephi 17:36–38; 21:1; 2 Nephi 10:20–22.) Through this means eventually all the families of the earth will be blessed—either through being of the blood of Abraham themselves, or through being ministered to by the blood of Abraham—with the right to the gospel, the priesthood, and eternal life. (See Pearl of Great Price, Abraham 2:8–11.)

On the other hand, the *gathering* of Israel is accomplished through repentance and turning to the Lord. Individuals were gathered in ancient days when they aligned themselves with the people of God, with those who practiced the religion of Jehovah and received the ordinances of salvation. They were gathered when they gained a sense of covenant identity, when they came to know who they were and whose they were. They were gathered when they congregated with the Former-day Saints, when they settled on those lands that were designated as promised lands—lands set apart as sacred sites for people of promise. The hope of the chosen people from Adam to Jacob, and the longing of the house of Israel from Joseph to Malachi, was to be reunited with their God and to enjoy fellowship with those of the household of faith. "But now thus saith the Lord that created thee, O Jacob," Isaiah recorded, "and he that formed thee, O Israel, Fear not: for I have redeemed thee, I have called thee by thy name; thou art mine."

> When thou passest through the waters, I will be with thee; and through the rivers, they shall not overflow thee; when thou walkest through the fire, thou shalt not be burned; neither shall the flame kindle upon thee.
> For I am the Lord thy God, the Holy One of Israel, thy Saviour. . . .
> Since thou wast precious in my sight, thou hast been honourable, and I have loved thee: therefore will I give men for thee, and people for thy life.
> Fear not: for I am with thee: I will bring thy seed from the east, and gather thee from the west;
> I will say to the north, Give up; and to the south, Keep not back: bring my sons from far, and my daughters from the ends of the earth. (Isaiah 43:1–6.)

"Ye shall be gathered one by one, O ye children of Israel," Isaiah declared. (Isaiah 27:12.) The call to the dispersed of Israel has been and ever will be the same: "Turn, O backsliding children, saith the Lord, for I am married unto you: and I will take you one of a city, and two of a family, and I will bring you to Zion." (Jeremiah 3:14.) That is to say, Latter-day Saints teach that gathering is accomplished through individual conversion, through faith, repentance, baptism, reception of the Holy Ghost, and the acceptance of and obedience to the ordinances of the holy temple.

Indeed, the Old Testament and Book of Mormon prophets longed for the day when the scattered remnants of Israel—those lost as to their identity and lost as to their relationship with the true Messiah and his church and kingdom—would be a part of a work that would cause all former gatherings to pale into insignificance. "Therefore, behold," Jeremiah recorded, "the days come, saith the Lord, that it shall no more be said, The Lord liveth, that brought up the children of Israel out of the land of Egypt; but, The Lord liveth, that brought up the children of Israel from the land of the north, and from all the lands whither he had driven them." And how is such a phenomenal gathering to be accomplished? "Behold, I will send for many fishers, saith the Lord, and they shall fish them; and after will I send for many hunters, and they shall hunt them from every mountain, and from every hill, and out of the holes of the rocks." (Jeremiah 16:14–16.) Latter-day Saints sense that through the great missionary work of the Church, they seek and teach and baptize and thereby gather the strangers home.

The crowning tie to Israel, however, comes only by the worthy reception of the blessings of the temple, through being endowed and sealed in family units. (See D&C 131:1–4.) "What was the [ultimate] object," Joseph Smith asked, "of gathering the Jews, or the people of God, in any age of the world?" He then answered: *The main object was to build unto the Lord a house whereby He could reveal unto His people the ordinances of His house and the glories of His kingdom,* and teach the people the way of salvation; for there are certain ordinances and principles that, when they are taught and practiced, must be done in a place or house built for that purpose."[14] "Missionary work," Russell M. Nelson observed, "is only the beginning" to the blessings of Abraham, Isaac, and Jacob. "The fulfillment, the consummation, of these blessings comes as those who have entered the waters of baptism perfect their lives to the point that they may enter the holy temple.

---

[14] *Teachings,* pp. 307–8; emphasis added.

Receiving an endowment there seals members of the Church to the Abrahamic Covenant."[15]

THE CALL OF A MODERN ABRAHAM

In September of 1823 the angel Moroni appeared to the Prophet Joseph Smith. "This messenger proclaimed himself," Joseph wrote, "to be an angel of God, sent to bring the joyful tidings that the covenant which God made with ancient Israel was at hand to be fulfilled, that the preparatory work for the second coming of the Messiah was speedily to commence; that the time was at hand for the Gospel in all its fulness to be preached in power, unto all nations that a people might be prepared for the Millennial reign. I was informed that I was chosen to be an instrument in the hands of God to bring about some of His purposes in this glorious dispensation."[16] The early leaders of the LDS Church taught that Joseph Smith was a descendant of Abraham. (See D&C 86:8–10; 124:58; 132:31, 49.) By lineage he had a right to the priesthood, the gospel, and eternal life. (See Pearl of Great Price, Abraham 2:8–11.)

One of the most fascinating parts of LDS theology follows on the heels of the above: what is true in regard to Joseph Smith's lineage—his right to the priesthood and the gospel, and his duty in regard to the salvation of the world—is equally true for all others who receive the covenant gospel and the sacraments or ordinances of salvation. A modern revelation thus speaks of the Latter-day Saints as "a remnant of Jacob, and those who are heirs according to the covenant." (D&C 52:2.) "Awake, awake; put on thy strength, O Zion," Isaiah recorded; "put on thy beautiful garments, O Jerusalem, the holy city." (Isaiah 52:1.) Joseph Smith recorded the following commentary: Jehovah "had reference to those whom God should call in the last days, who should hold the power of priesthood to bring again Zion, and the redemption

---

[15] "Thanks for the Covenant," p. 59.
[16] *History of the Church* 4:536–37.

of Israel; and to put on her strength is to put on the authority of the priesthood, which she, Zion, has a right to by lineage; also to return to that power which she had lost." (D&C 113:8.) The Lord encouraged Israel through Isaiah to shake herself from the dust and loose herself from the bands about her neck. (Isaiah 52:2.) That is, "the scattered remnants are exhorted to return to the Lord from whence they have fallen; which if they do, the promise of the Lord is that he will speak to them, or give them revelation." In so doing, Israel rids herself of "the curses of God upon her," her "scattered condition among the Gentiles." (D&C 113:10.)

Mormons believe that Joseph Smith became a "father of the faithful" to those of this dispensation, the means by which the chosen people could be identified, gathered, organized as family units, and sealed forevermore into the house of Israel to their God. Joseph Smith explained that on April 3, 1836, Moses appeared in the temple in Kirtland, Ohio, and restored the keys (directing power) of the gathering of Israel. A messenger named Elias then committed unto Joseph and Oliver Cowdery the "dispensation of the gospel of Abraham," making it possible that through those first elders all generations after them would be blessed. (Compare Genesis 17:1–7.) That is, Elias restored the power necessary to organize eternal family units through the new and everlasting covenant of marriage. Joseph Smith said that Elijah then appeared and restored the power to bind and seal those family units for eternity, as well as the power to legitimize all priesthood sacraments and give them efficacy, virtue, and force in and after the resurrection. (D&C 110:11–15.)

THE FUTURE

Latter-day Saints believe that the gathering of Israel entails more than a movement of Jews to the Holy Land. From an LDS perspective, the Jews are indeed God's chosen people, but they are only one branch of many branches of the whole house of Israel. The LDS prophetic picture is one of increased numbers of people joining the Church and thus coming into the covenant, a gathering of more and more of Abraham's descendants—who are scattered throughout the world—unto the God of their fathers. What the Book of Mormon calls "the work of the Father"—the work of gathering Israel into the fold—though begun in the early nineteenth century, will continue into and through the Millennium. In that glorious era of peace and righteousness, the dispersed of Israel will receive the message of truth, traverse the "highway of righteousness" (Isaiah 35:8) into the true fold, and take their place beside their kinsmen in the household of faith. Truly, "such of the gathering of Israel as has come to pass so far is but the gleam of a star that soon will be hidden by the splendor of the sun in full blaze; truly, the magnitude and grandeur and glory of the gathering is yet to be."[17]

The Church of Jesus Christ of Latter-day Saints declares that the prophecy of Jeremiah, partially fulfilled in the coming of Jesus to earth, will have its ultimate realization in the Millennium. "Behold," Jeremiah wrote, "the days come, saith the Lord, that I will make a new covenant with the house of Israel, and with the house of Judah:"

> Not according to the covenant that I made with their fathers in the day that I took them by the hand to bring them out of the land of Egypt; which my covenant they brake, although I was an husband unto them, saith the Lord:
>
> But this shall be the covenant that I will make with the house of Israel; after those days, saith the Lord, I will put my law in their inward parts, and write it in their hearts; and will be their God, and they shall be my people.
>
> And they shall teach no more every man his neighbour, and every man his brother, saying, Know the Lord: for they shall all know me, from the least of them unto the greatest of them, saith the Lord: for I will forgive their iniquity, and I will remember their sin no more. (Jeremiah 31:31–34.)

---

[17] Bruce R. McConkie, *The Millennial Messiah: The Second Coming of the Son of Man* (Salt Lake City: Deseret Book Co., 1982), p. 196.

CHAPTER 11

REASON, REVELATION, AND THE DEVOTIONAL LIFE

One of the purposes of this life is to continue our growth toward God and godliness. In doing so, men and women are expected to use their heart, might, mind, and strength. The Almighty is to be approached and served through the intelligent application of divine truths, through a mature cultivation of both mind and heart, through reason and revelation.

SPIRITUALITY

For Joseph Smith, spirituality was a state of being, a condition achieved through the merging of the temporal and the spiritual, the finite and the infinite. Spirituality was essentially the result of a righteous life coupled with heightened perspective, an increased sensitivity to the things of God among men. To possess spirituality was to recognize that in the end all things are spiritual and that God has never given a purely temporal (time-bound or temporary) command or directive. In this sense, the Latter-day Saints seek to reconcile the irreconcilable. Indeed, the growth and spread of the Church may be attributed largely to what some might consider to be competing or contradictory processes: (1) constancy and adherence to "the ancient order of things"; and (2) development and change, according to needs and circumstances. The LDS faith may thus be characterized as a religious culture with both static and dynamic, priestly and prophetic elements, a movement acclimated to both conservative and progressive postures. Joseph Smith held tenaciously to and grounded his people in what he believed to be the particular beliefs and rites of both ancient Israel and first-century Christianity. At the same time, because of their belief in modern and continuing revelation, the LDS people have sought for and welcomed new developments and changes as such have seemed essential to the perpetuity of the Saints' vision of the holy city.

Spirituality consisted of tying the heavens to the earth, imbuing man with the powers of God, and thereby elevating society. Such a change in one's nature was to be undertaken "in the world," amid the throes of spiritual opposition; one need not resort to monasticism in order to come out of the world. It was to be accomplished by every man and woman, not just priest or minister, "for God hath not revealed anything to Joseph, but what He will make known unto the Twelve [Apostles], and even the least saint may know all things as fast as he is able to bear them."[1] Brigham Young spoke of Joseph Smith's ability to communicate spiritual matters:

> When I saw Joseph Smith, he took heaven, figuratively speaking, and brought it down to earth; and he took earth, brought it up, and opened up, in plainness and simplicity, the things of God. The excellency of the glory of the character of Brother Joseph Smith was that he could reduce heavenly things to the understanding of the finite. When he preached to the people—revealed the things of God, the

---

[1] *Teachings*, p. 149.

will of God, the plan of salvation, the purposes of Jehovah, the relation in which we stand to Him and all the heavenly things—he reduced his teachings to the capacity of every man, woman, and child, making them as plain as a well-defined pathway. . . .

When you hear a man pour out eternal things, how [good] you feel! To what nearness you seem to be brought to God! What a delight it was to hear Brother Joseph talk upon the great principles of eternity![2]

David O. McKay, ninth president of the LDS Church, explained that spirituality is "the consciousness of victory over self, and of communion with the Infinite. Spirituality impels one to conquer difficulties and acquire more and more strength. To feel one's faculties unfolding and truth expanding the soul is one of life's sublimest experiences."[3] This statement is a distillation expression characterizing an LDS view of the spiritual and contemplative life. Mormons believe that men and women are literally the spirit children of God the Father, that God is in reality an exalted man, a Man of Holiness, and that men and women are thus of the same species as their Creator. Men and women are to pray to their Maker as "Our Father in heaven" and mean what they pray.

Latter-day Saints believe that "communion with the Infinite" is to be accomplished most often through personal prayer. Members of the faith are encouraged to pray on their knees morning and night, and in their hearts at other times throughout the day. They are instructed to pray to the Father, in the name of the Son, by the power of the Holy Ghost. Joseph Smith himself taught and demonstrated that prayers should be simple and direct, never ostentatious or delivered for any reason other than to communicate with and petition one's God. One member of the Church recalled, "Speaking about praying to our Father in heaven, I once heard Joseph Smith remark, 'Be plain and simple, and ask for what you

---

[2] A combined expression of Brigham Young from three separate addresses; in *Journal of Discourses* 4:54; 5:332; 8:206.

[3] *Gospel Ideals* (Salt Lake City: The Improvement Era, 1953), p. 390.

want, just like you would go to a neighbor and say, I want to borrow your horse to go to the mill.'"[4] Earnest and sincere prayers are rewarded. "The Spirit shall be given unto you by the prayer of faith." (D&C 42:14.)

REASON AND REVELATION

From the time of his First Vision in the spring of 1820 until the time of his death, Joseph Smith declared that revelation is essential to the highest of eternal opportunities: "Salvation cannot come without revelation; it is vain for anyone to minister without it."[5] Joseph stressed that revelation—communion with the Almighty—is as essential to individual growth and salvation as it is to institutional growth and perpetuation: "No man can receive the Holy Ghost without receiving revelations. The Holy Ghost is a revelator."[6]

On the relationship between our rational faculties—the power of reason—and our spiritual capacities—the place of revelation—a modern apostle, Dallin H. Oaks, has written, "Reason is a thinking process using facts and logic that can be communicated to another person and tested by objective (that is, measurable) criteria. Revelation is communication from God to man. It cannot be defined and tested like reason. Reason involves thinking and demonstrating. Revelation involves hearing or seeing or understanding or feeling. Reason is potentially public. Revelation is invariably personal." Then, in stressing the innate limitations upon reason, he continued, "Despite the importance of study and reason, if we seek to learn of the things of God solely by this method, we are certain to stop short of our goal. We may even wind up at the wrong destination. Why is this so? On this subject God has prescribed the primacy of another method. To learn the things of God, what we need is not more study and reason,

---

[4] As cited in *They Knew the Prophet*, compiled by Hyrum L. and Helen Mae Andrus (Salt Lake City: Bookcraft, 1974), p. 100.
[5] *Teachings*, p. 160.
[6] Ibid., p. 328.

not more scholarship and technology, but more faith and revelation."[7]

For the Latter-day Saints, however, revelation does not represent a mystical distancing of oneself from reality, a transcendental separation of one's reason from the receipt of a revelation. The will of God is meant to be understood and to be as satisfying to the mind as it is soothing to the heart. Latter-day Saints are never instructed to give themselves wholly to feelings any more than they are instructed to surrender all thought. In a revelation given to Joseph Smith and an early Church leader, Oliver Cowdery, in April of 1829, are found these words: "Yea, behold, I will tell you in your mind and in your heart, by the Holy Ghost, which shall come upon you and which shall dwell in your heart." (D&C 8:2.) Joseph F. McConkie, a professor of religion at Brigham Young University, has commented on this passage:

> We observe that neither [Oliver Cowdery] nor Joseph was to experience any suspension of their natural faculties in the process of obtaining revelation. Quite to the contrary, their hearts and minds were to be the very media through which the revelation came. Prophets are not hollow shells through which the voice of the Lord echoes, nor are they mechanical recording devices; prophets are men of passion, feeling, intellect. One does not suspend agency, mind, or spirit in the service of God. It is . . . with heart, might, mind and strength that we have been asked to serve, and in nothing is this more apparent than the receiving of revelation. There is no mindless worship or service in the kingdom of heaven.[8]

Frequently members of the LDS Church are encouraged by their leaders to utilize a pattern for revelation in the resolution of personal problems—they are to study out the alter-

---

[7] *The Lord's Way* (Salt Lake City: Deseret Book Co., 1991), pp. 16–17, 19.

[8] "The Principle of Revelation," in *Studies in Scripture Vol. 1: The Doctrine and Covenants,* edited by Robert L. Millet and Kent P. Jackson (Salt Lake City: Deseret Book Co., 1989), p. 83.

natives, make an intelligent choice, and then present the same to God in prayer for his confirmation or rejection. (See D&C 9:7–9.)

Latter-day Saints believe that faith has its own type of discipline. Some things that are obvious to the faithful sound like the gibberish of alien tongues to the faithless. The discipline of faith, the concentrated and consecrated effort to become single to God, has its own reward, a reward that includes the expansion of the mind. Those who follow such discipline come to be filled with light and are able in time to "comprehend all things." (D&C 88:67.) It is worth considering the words of a revelation given in Kirtland, Ohio. The early Saints were told: "As all have not faith, seek ye diligently and teach one another words of wisdom; yea, seek ye out of the best books words of wisdom; seek learning, even by study and also by faith." (D&C 88:118.) We note that the counsel to seek learning out of the best books is prefaced by the negative clause, "As all *have not* faith . . ." One wonders whether what was not intended was something like the following: Since all do not have sufficient faith—have not "matured in their religious convictions"[9] to learn by any other means—then they must seek learning by study, through the use of the rational processes. Perhaps learning by studying from the best books would then be greatly enhanced by revelation. Latter-day Saints believe that honest truth seekers may learn things in this way that they could not know otherwise. This may be what Joseph Smith meant when he taught that "the best way to obtain truth and wisdom is not to ask it from books, but to go to God in prayer, and obtain divine teaching."[10] It is surely in this same context that another of the Prophet's famous yet little-understood statements finds meaning: "Could you gaze into heaven five minutes," he declared, "you would know more than you would by reading all that ever was written on the

---

[9] B. H. Roberts, as cited by Harold B. Lee in Conference Report, April 1968, p. 129.
[10] *Teachings*, p. 191.

subject" of life after death.[11] "I believe in study," Marion G. Romney, a member of the Church's First Presidency for many years, stated. "I believe that men learn much through study. As a matter of fact, it has been my observation that they learn little concerning things as they are, as they were, or as they are to come without study. *I also believe, however, and know, that learning by study is greatly accelerated by faith."*[12]

Harold B. Lee, eleventh president of the Church, expressed the following to Brigham Young University students just weeks before his death in 1973: "The acquiring of knowledge by faith is no easy road to learning. It will demand strenuous effort and continual striving by faith. In short, learning by faith is no task for a lazy man. Someone has said, in effect, that 'such a process requires the bending of the whole soul, the calling up from the depths of the human mind and linking the person with God. The right connection must be formed; then only comes knowledge by faith, a kind of knowledge that goes beyond secular learning, that reaches into the realms of the unknown and makes those who follow that course great in the sight of the Lord.'"[13] On another occasion, President Lee taught that "learning by faith requires *the bending of the whole soul through worthy living to become attuned to the Holy Spirit of the Lord,* the calling up from the depths of one's own mental searching, and the linking of our own efforts to receive the true witness of the Spirit."[14]

GROWING IN SPIRITUAL GRACES

Latter-day Saints believe that the most universal form of revelation is what they call the Light of Christ. The Light of Christ is a light that dwells within every person born into this world. (John 1:9; D&C 84:46–47.) In a sense the Light of

[11] Ibid., p. 324.
[12] *Learning for the Eternities* (Salt Lake City: Deseret Book Co., 1977), p. 72; emphasis added.
[13] "Be Loyal to the Royal within You," *1973 BYU Speeches of the Year* (Provo: BYU Publications, 1974), p. 91.
[14] Conference Report, April 1971, p. 94; emphasis added.

Christ might be viewed as light along a grand continuum. On one end of this continuum (the "less refined" realm) is the light of the sun, moon, and stars, the physical light that allows us to see and live and function, as well as the light that constitutes the laws and powers of nature by which order in the cosmos is maintained. On the other end of the continuum (the "more refined" realm) are the revelatory, cleansing, and regenerating powers of the Spirit. This Light of Christ therefore has both natural and redemptive functions—it is the source of light for photosynthesis, the source of light for instinct in animals, and the source of reason, understanding, innate moral awareness, and revelation in men and women.[15]

One Church leader has explained:

> As part of life itself, all mortals are endowed with a heavenly gift called the light of Christ. This divine endowment manifests to us the difference between good and evil. We do not need to be taught what is right and wrong. This knowledge is bred in our bones; it is hereditary; it is innate, inborn, and intuitional in nature. Call it conscience, if you will; say that it is a divine inheritance from a Divine Parent; identify it as a spark of divinity sent by Deity to fire the soul with the flames of righteousness. . . .
>
> The light of Christ, conforming to the will of that God whose influence and spirit it is, dwells in the hearts of all men. If it were not present, life would cease, for it is the light of life as that life comes from God. It is the instrumentality and agency by which Deity keeps in touch and communes with all his children, both the righteous and the wicked. It has an edifying, enlightening, and uplifting influence on men. . . .
>
> It is the means by which the Lord invites and entices all men to improve their lot and to come unto him and receive his gospel. It is the agency through which the Lord strives

---

[15] See Parley P. Pratt, *Key to the Science of Theology,* 1978 ed., p. 25; Charles W. Penrose, *Journal of Discourses* 26:21–23; Marion G. Romney, Conference Report, April 1977, pp. 59–63; Bruce R. McConkie, *A New Witness for the Articles of Faith,* pp. 45, 70, 257–59, 309.

with men, through which he encourages them to forsake the world and come unto Christ, through which good desires and feelings are planted in the hearts of decent people. It is the medium of intelligence that guides inventors, scientists, artists, composers, poets, authors, statesmen, philosophers, generals, leaders, and influential men in general, when they set their hands to do that which is for the benefit and blessing of their fellowmen. By it the Lord guides in the affairs of men and directs the courses of nations and kingdoms.[16]

Again, all men and women are entitled to the Light of Christ. Those who hearken to the voice of conscience, who earnestly seek to be true to moral values, will be led to the greater light of the Holy Ghost—the right to a more intense and constant instruction and sanctifying power—within the covenant gospel, either in this life or the next.[17]

Jesus instructed his disciples after his resurrection, "Go ye into all the world, and preach the gospel to every creature. He that believeth and is baptized shall be saved; but he that believeth not shall be damned. And these signs shall follow them that believe; in my name shall they cast out devils; they shall speak with new tongues; they shall take up serpents; and if they drink any deadly thing, it shall not hurt them: they shall lay hands on the sick, and they shall recover." (Mark 16:15–18.) The Latter-day Saints believe that one of the signs of Christ's Church is the gifts of the Spirit, those wonders and miracles that characterized the faithful in generations past. "We believe in the gift of tongues, prophecy, revelation, visions, healing, interpretation of tongues, and so forth." (Pearl of Great Price, Articles of Faith 1:7.) Latter-day Saints believe that whenever the powers and truths of salvation are on earth, then the signs of the faith—so clearly discussed in the New Testament (1 Corinthians 12)—follow naturally. Faith itself is not established by miracles or physical evidence alone, but signs follow those that believe. (See D&C 63:7–12.)

---

[16] Bruce R. McConkie, *A New Witness for the Articles of Faith*, pp. 45, 258–59.
[17] See D&C 84:47–48; Joseph F. Smith, *Gospel Doctrine*, pp. 67–68.

Though it is true that members of The Church of Jesus Christ of Latter-day Saints believe strongly in miracles and in God's ability to heal and lift and strengthen through spiritual gifts, yet they are cautious as to the visibility of the gifts. They sense that sacred matters are to be spoken of and participated in reverently and without fanfare. It is thus the case that while tens of thousands of Latter-day Saints will express an intense faith in spiritual gifts and the working of miracles— many of these same people testifying that they have thereby been the recipient of God's mercy and healing grace—they are cautious about sensationalism and sensitive about public display or advertisement.

Paul taught that the things of God can be discerned and known only by the Spirit of God. (1 Corinthians 2:11–14.) "Nothing is a greater injury to the children of men," Joseph Smith said, "than to be under the influence of a false spirit when they think they have the Spirit of God."[18] The powers of God ought to bring honor and glory to God, and thus any action that detracts from the divine dignity of the Almighty is suspect. There is "nothing indecorous" in the doings of God, and that "there is nothing unnatural in the Spirit of God."[19]

Both the Book of Mormon (Moroni 10) and the Doctrine and Covenants (section 46) provide listings of the gifts of the Spirit. Both stress, with the Apostle Paul (1 Corinthians 12), that these gifts are provided by God as a reward to the faithful, a blessing to the believers, that they are as parts of the body of Christ, all of which are essential to a functioning and dynamic church. In addition, they are given to help members of the body of Christ avoid deception:

> Beware lest ye are deceived; and that ye may not be deceived seek ye earnestly the best gifts, always remembering for what they are given;
> For verily I say unto you, they are given for the benefit of those who love me and keep all my commandments, and him that seeketh so to do; that all may be benefited that

---

[18] *Teachings*, p. 205.
[19] Ibid., pp. 209, 214.

seek or that ask of me, that ask and not for a sign that they may consume it upon their lusts.

And again, verily I say unto you, I would that ye should always remember, and always retain in your minds what those gifts are, that are given unto the church.

For all have not every gift given unto them; for there are many gifts, and to every man is given a gift by the Spirit of God.

To some is given one, and to some is given another, that all may be profited thereby.

Then follows the recitation of such gifts as the testimony of Jesus, the gifts of administration, wisdom, knowledge, faith to be healed, faith to heal, miracles, prophecy, discernment, tongues, and the interpretation of tongues. (D&C 46:8–25; compare Book of Mormon, Moroni 10:8–18.)

The Latter-day Saints are taught to purify their hearts and minds of all duplicity or double-mindedness; to consecrate and prioritize their lives in such a way that they are not seduced by worldly attachments that too often dilute their Christian discipleship; and to avoid moral pollution, harshness, crudeness, or any such thing that would desensitize them to matters of eternal worth. Further, they are instructed to pray with all the energy of their hearts to be endowed with the gifts of the Spirit and the fruit of the Spirit—"love, joy, peace, longsuffering, gentleness, goodness, faith, meekness, temperance." That is, they are counseled regularly to "live in the Spirit," that they might thereby "walk in the Spirit." (Galatians 5:22–23, 25; compare Book of Mormon, Moroni 7:48.)

Joseph Smith taught that one of the greatest revelations a man or woman could receive was the peaceful assurance that the tests in mortality had been passed, that the Lord was pleased with one's performance in life, and that exaltation—the glory and life associated with the highest heaven hereafter—was a reality. To receive such an assurance was to receive the promise of eternal life.[20] Traditional Protestant Christians

---

[20] See 2 Peter 1; see also *Teachings,* pp. 149–51, 298–301.

speak of "being saved" at the time they accept Jesus Christ as Savior. Similarly, the Latter-day Saints believe that receiving a testimony that God is our Father and Jesus is the Christ is fundamental and foundational to one's faith. But the quest for righteousness through Christian service, relying upon the mercy and grace of Jesus, allows people to know, through the peaceful presence and comfort of the Holy Spirit throughout their lives, that they are on course, in covenant, and that the Lord is pleased. *"It is present salvation and the present influence of the Holy Ghost that we need every day to keep us on saving ground,"* Brigham Young declared.

> When an individual refuses to comply with the further requirements of heaven, then . . . his former righteousness departs from him, and is not accounted to him for righteousness: but *if he had continued in righteousness and obedience to the requirements of heaven, he is saved all the time, through baptism, the laying on of hands, and obeying the commandments of the Lord and all that is required of him by the heavens—the living oracles. He is saved now, next week, next year, and continually, and is prepared for the celestial kingdom of God whenever the time comes for him to inherit it.*
>
> *I want present salvation.* I preach, comparatively, but little about the eternities and Gods, and their wonderful works in eternity; and do not tell who first made them, nor how they were made; for I know nothing about that. *Life is for us, and it is for us to receive today, and not wait for the millennium. Let us take a course to be saved today,* and, when evening comes, review the acts of the day, repent of our sins, if we have any to repent of, and say our prayers; then we can lie down and sleep in peace until the morning, arise with gratitude to God, commence the labours of another day, and strive to live the whole day to God and nobody else.[21]

Devoting oneself to the service of God and the blessing of mankind entails yielding one's heart unto God and consecrating one's faculties to higher ideals. Spirituality thus becomes a

---

[21] *Journal of Discourses* 8:124–25; emphasis added.

process, a focused journey from the finite to the infinite, but a journey whose sublime by-products are worth the struggle. As Joseph Smith stated:

> We consider that God has created man with a mind capable of instruction, and a faculty which may be enlarged in proportion to the heed and diligence given to the light communicated from heaven to the intellect; and that the nearer man approaches perfection, the clearer are his views, and the greater his enjoyments, till he has overcome the evils of his life and lost every desire for sin; and like the ancients, arrives at that point of faith where he is wrapped in the power and glory of his Maker and is caught up to dwell with Him.[22]

***

[22] *Teachings,* p. 51.

CHAPTER 12

THE GOOD LIFE

U p to this point we have dealt almost exclusively with LDS theology. In this chapter we will comment briefly on some of the more visible aspects of The Church of Jesus Christ of Latter-day Saints, about the lifestyle and fruits of the faith.

ETHICS FLOW FROM THEOLOGY

The Latter-day Saints do not believe that their actions in society, and any good that may come from Christian labors, can be separated from their doctrine. To begin with, Latter-day Saints believe that a people cannot really be built upon Christ's gospel if they do not believe in the divinity of Jesus Christ. Those who labor tirelessly to lighten burdens or alleviate human suffering, but at the same time deny the fact that Jesus Christ is God, cannot have the lasting impact on society that they could have through drawing upon those spiritual forces that center in the Lord. Those in our day who focus endlessly on the moral teachings of Jesus but who downplay the divine Sonship miss the mark.

For some people, Jesus stands as the preeminent example of kindness, the ultimate illustration of social and interpersonal graciousness and morality. A favorite text for this group is the Sermon on the Mount, while their highest aspiration is the call to live the Golden Rule. A Roman Catholic philosopher has observed, "According to the theological liberal, [the Sermon on the Mount] is the essence of Christianity, and Christ is the best of human teachers and examples. . . . Christianity is essentially ethics. What's missing here?" he asks. "Simply, the essence of Christianity, which is *not* the Sermon on the Mount. When Christianity was proclaimed throughout the world, the proclamation (*kerygma*) was not 'Love your enemies!' but 'Christ is risen!' This was not a new *ideal* but a new *event*, that God became man, died, and rose for our salvation. Christianity is first of all not ideal but real, an event, news, the gospel, the 'good news.' The essence of Christianity is not Christianity; the essence of Christianity is Christ."[1]

For many, the doctrine of Christ has been replaced by the ethics of Jesus. Those who insist that ethics must be taught or stressed point toward the declining moral standards of our day, the increase of drug abuse or teenage pregnancy, the prevalence of our inhumanity to each other. They contend that if Christianity is to make a difference in the world, we must find ways to transform ethereal theology into religious practice in a decaying society. They thus seek to promote a social gospel, a relevant religion. The problem with a social gospel, for the Latter-day Saints, is that it is inherently deficient as far as engaging the real problems of human beings. It almost always focuses on symptoms rather than causes. Ethics is not the essence of the gospel. Ethics is not necessarily righteousness. The very word *ethics* has come to connote socially acceptable standards based on current consensus, as opposed to absolute truths based on God's eternal laws. Ethics is too often to virtue and righteousness what theology is to religion—a pale and powerless substitute. Indeed, ethics without the virtue that comes through the cleansing powers of the Redeemer is like religion without God, at least the true and living God.

---

[1] Peter Kreeft, *Back to Virtue* (San Francisco: Ignatius Press, 1992), p. 83.

"It is one thing," Bruce R. McConkie has written, "to teach ethical principles, quite another to proclaim the great doctrinal verities, which are the foundation of true Christianity and out of which eternal salvation comes. True it is that salvation is limited to those in whose souls the ethical principles abound, but true it is also that Christian ethics, in the full and saving sense, automatically become a part of the lives of those who first believe Christian doctrines." In summary, "It is only when gospel ethics are tied to gospel doctrines that they rest on a sure and enduring foundation and gain full operation in the lives of the saints."[2] The Latter-day Saints are occasionally criticized for expending so much of the resources of the Church on missionary work or the construction of temples. Some say that the institutional Church should be more involved in leading or officially supporting this or that crusade, in laboring for this or that social cause. "Where is your charity?" they ask. "Of what avail are your noble theological principles?"

I agree with Bruce Hafen, who pointed out, "The ultimate purpose of the gospel of Jesus Christ is to cause the sons and daughters of God to become as Christ is. Those who see religious purpose only in terms of ethical service in the relationship between man and fellowmen may miss that divinely ordained possibility. It is quite possible to render charitable— even 'Christian'—service without developing deeply ingrained and permanent Christlike character. Paul understood this when he warned against giving all one's goods to feed the poor without charity. . . . *While religious philosophies whose highest aim is social relevance may do much good, they will not ultimately lead people to achieve the highest religious purpose, which is to become as God and Christ are.*"[3] Latter-day Saints believe that when people have been true to their trusts and live worthy of the gifts and influence of the Holy Ghost, then the works of the Father—the works of righteousness, the actions and behaviors of the faithful, including deeds of Christian

---

[2] *A New Witness for the Articles of Faith,* pp. 699–700.
[3] *The Broken Heart,* pp. 196–97.

service—flow forth from regenerate hearts. Those works are not just the works of mortals but rather the doings of people who have become new creatures in Christ. Their works are therefore the works of the Lord, for they have been motivated by the power of his Spirit. To the Philippian Saints the Apostle Paul beckoned, "Work out your own salvation with fear and trembling. For *it is God which worketh in you* both to will and to do of his good pleasure." (Philippians 2:12–13; emphasis added.)

In short, Latter-day Saints believe that only when ethical behaviors are founded on theology will the change in individuals and society be lasting. As a modern apostle observed, "True doctrine, understood, changes attitudes and behavior. The study of the doctrines of the gospel will improve behavior quicker than a study of behavior will improve behavior. Preoccupation with unworthy behavior can lead to unworthy behavior. That is why we stress so forcefully the study of the doctrines of the gospel."[4]

FRUITS OF THE FAITH

Like members of all churches, the Latter-day Saints try their best to live their religion but fall short occasionally. They teach and reach toward the ideal, but the ideal is still, with many, an unblemished reality. Nevertheless, some things do seem to work.

Focus on Families. For one thing, the LDS belief in the plan of salvation puts tremendous stress upon the family as the most important unit in time or eternity. Families, not classes, are saved and exalted. Families, not church groups, are saved. "The home is the basis of a righteous life, and no other instrumentality can take its place, nor fulfill its essential functions."[5] Neal A. Maxwell, a modern Church leader warned the Latter-day Saints that "healthy, traditional families are becoming an endangered species! Perhaps, one day, families

---

[4] Boyd K. Packer, in Conference Report, October 1986, p. 20.
[5] David O. McKay, in *Family Home Evening Manual* (Salt Lake City: The Church of Jesus Christ of Latter-day Saints, 1965), preface.

may even rank with the threatened spotted owl in effective attention given!" He continued:

> When parents fail to transmit testimony and theology along with decency, those families are only one generation from serious spiritual decline, having lost their savor. [See Matthew 5:13.] The law of the harvest [see Galatians 6:7–8] is nowhere more in evidence and nowhere more relentless than in family gardens! . . .
>
> Society should focus anew on the headwaters—the family—where values can be taught, lived, experienced, and perpetuated. Otherwise, brothers and sisters, we will witness even more widespread flooding downstream, featuring even more corruption and violence (see Genesis 6:11–12; Matthew 24:37). . . .
>
> As the number of dysfunctional families increases, their failures will spill into already burdened schools and streets. It is not a pretty scene even now.
>
> Nations in which traditional idealism gives way to modern cynicism will forfeit the blessings of heaven, which they so urgently need, and such nations will also lose legitimacy in the eyes of their citizens.[6]

Anticipating attacks on the family, in the 1960s a general directive from Church headquarters asked that Monday evenings be set aside by all members for family home evening. No church meetings or group activities were to be scheduled. The family home evening is to be a time for gospel instruction as well as social activity. It is a time for the family to put aside work, school, and pressures and focus on the things that matter most—parents and children, fathers and mothers, brothers and sisters. In addition, parents have been encouraged, as mentioned in chapter 8, to read the scriptures and hold regular family devotionals, pray, and communicate meaningfully with their children. Family togetherness and family religious observance are intended to instill within the children the need for individual involvement with spiritual things.

---

[6] Conference Report, April 1994, p. 119–22.

To be sure, Mormons struggle to hold their families together, just as do people of other faiths. But on the whole, studies show that LDS young people, especially those who have incorporated the teachings of the Church and the family—those who engage in private religious behavior—are much less prone to delinquency than other youth. The young people studied "appear to have internalized a set of religious values and practices that are related to less frequent participation in delinquent activity in both high and low moral communities. The relationship of religion with delinquency for this population is not entirely a cultural or social phenomenon. The link between religion and delinquency was just as robust in the low-LDS religious climate of the eastern states as it was in the powerful religious environments of Southern California, Idaho, and Utah."[7]

Marriage and Divorce. Latter-day Saints believe there is a commitment to the marriage union, a commitment to family life, and a commitment to Christian principles that flow from the ennobling concept of the eternal family. Once a couple realizes that their covenant with each other and God is eternal, intended to span the veil of death and transcend time, then they can hardly view one another in quite the same way. Small provocations between marriage partners, for example, seldom result in serious discussions about divorce, inasmuch as marriage and family have been exalted beyond the realm of social dynamics to that of an everlasting religious institution. One sociologist commented:

> Mormons are more likely than other groups to marry; they are less likely to divorce; if they do divorce, they are more likely to remarry; and they are likely to bear a larger number of children. On each measure [of the study performed], there is a clearly-defined impact associated with

---

[7] Bruce A. Chadwick and Brent L. Top, "Religiosity and Delinquency among LDS Adolescents," *Journal for the Scientific Study of Religion,* vol. 32, no. 1, 1993, pp. 51–67; see also Brent L. Top and Bruce A. Chadwick, "The Power of the Word: Religion, Family, Friends, and Delinquent Behavior of LDS Youth," *Brigham Young University Studies,* vol. 33, no. 2, 1993, pp. 293–310.

one's religious affiliation. Those with no religion are generally least likely to marry, most likely to divorce if they marry, least likely to remarry following a divorce, and most likely to have the smallest family size. . . . Among Latter-day Saints, differences between temple and nontemple marriages enlarge the differences between frequent and infrequent attenders at religious services. Temple marriages are characterized by lower divorce rates and larger family sizes. Non-temple marriages are almost five times more likely to result in divorce than are temple marriages.[8]

Education and Religiosity. For some time now, studies have indicated that higher education tends to have a strong negative influence on religiosity. Various explanations have been offered, but perhaps the most popular is the secularizing effect of post–high-school study on one's commitment to the faith. The British physicist Paul Davies observed, "If the church is largely ignored today it is not because science has finally won its age-old battle with religion, but because it has so radically reoriented our society that the biblical perspective of the world now seems largely irrelevant."[9] A related explanation posits that "higher education tends to both expand one's horizons and increase exposure to countercultural values. Such exposure works to erode the traditional plausibility structures which maintain the poorly understood religious convictions so typical of American religion. In other words, poorly grounded religious beliefs have simply been unable to stand in the face of challenges generated by modern science and higher education."[10]

Since their beginnings, the Latter-day Saints have placed tremendous stress on the value of education; it is a religious principle that men and women should strive to gain all of the

---

[8] Stan L. Albrecht, "The Consequential Dimension of Mormon Religiosity," *Brigham Young University Studies,* vol. 29, no. 2, 1989, pp. 88, 91; see also Stan L. Albrecht and Howard M. Bahr, "Patterns of Religious Disaffiliation: A Study of Lifelong Mormons, Mormon Converts, and Former Mormons," *Journal for the Scientific Study of Religion,* vol. 22, no. 4, 1983, pp. 366–79.

[9] *God and the New Physics* (New York: Simon & Schuster, 1983), p. 2.

[10] Albrecht, "The Consequential Dimension to Mormon Religiosity," p. 100.

education and training possible to better themselves and their circumstances in life. Thus for both males and females, the percentage of Latter-day Saints who have completed post–high-school education or training is significantly higher than the nation as a whole. Research demonstrates that 53.5 percent of LDS males have some type of post–high-school education, compared to 36.5 for the U.S. population. For females, 44.3 percent have received some post–high-school education, 27.7 percent for the U.S. population. In addition, the Latter-day Saints defy the long-held thesis concerning higher education and religiosity. Weekly attendance at church for males works as follows: those with only a grade-school education attended 34 percent of the time, while LDS males with post–high-school education attended 80 percent of the meetings. The same results followed in such other areas of religiosity as financial contributions, frequency of personal prayer, and the frequency of personal scripture study. In short, the secularizing influence of higher education does not seem to hold for the Latter-day Saints.[11]

The Church Welfare Program. In the 1930s and during the time of the Great Depression, many members of the LDS Church found themselves in the same plight as their neighbors. The leader of one of the ecclesiastical units in Salt Lake City found, for example, that of the 7,300 people under his care, 4,800 were receiving some form of government welfare assistance. The leader, Harold B. Lee (who became the eleventh president of the Church in 1972), with his counselors, set about to establish a program of assistance for the members that would preserve their dignity and allow them to work for what they received. His welfare program was successful, was eventually implemented Churchwide, and he was asked to oversee what came to be known as the Church Welfare Services Program. The primary purpose of the program, as announced by Church leaders in 1936, was "to set up . . . a system under which the curse of idleness would be done

---

[11] See Stan L. Albrecht and Tim B. Heaton, "Secularization, Higher Education, and Religiosity," *Review of Religious Research,* vol. 26, no. 1, 1984, pp. 49–54.

away with, the evils of a dole abolished, and independence, industry, thrift, and self respect be once more established amongst our people. The aim of the Church is to help the people to help themselves. Work is to be reenthroned as the ruling principle of the lives of our Church membership."[12]

As mentioned in chapter 8, members of the Church are asked to pay 10 percent of their income as a tithing. These funds are used to build chapels and temples and to finance missionary service. In addition, members are asked to fast from food and drink (two meals) once per month and then to donate the equivalent cost to a fast offering to be used for the care of the poor. Those in need are expected to exhaust every personal, family, and extended family resource before turning to the Church; having surveyed all options, members should feel no hesitation in seeking temporary assistance from the Church as administered by the local bishop. This use of fast offerings is a vital part of the Church Welfare Program. Further, the Church maintains employment centers, as well as Social Services agencies that deal in foster care, unwed mother care, adoptions, and individual and family counseling. Helping members meet their needs entails more in this complex age than just seeing to a proper diet; social, emotional, occupational, and literacy needs are just as important, and so the Church maintains formal programs to help individuals and families become independent and self-reliant. Finally, it might be observed that through the fast offering program the LDS Church has in the past been able to send tons of supplies—food, clothing, bedding, and so on—to needy people (Mormon and non-Mormon) in such areas as Germany following World War II and, more recently, to many third-world countries.

The Health Code. In 1833 Joseph Smith introduced to the Church what has come to be known as the Word of Wisdom, a health code that the Saints believe has both physical and spiritual benefits. Believing that the body is the temple of God (1 Corinthians 3:16–17; 6:19–20), members are asked to

---

[12] Heber J. Grant, in Conference Report, October 1936, p. 3.

abstain from alcohol, tobacco, harmful drugs, coffee, and tea. Complete observance of the Word of Wisdom is considered requisite for good standing in the Church and admittance into temples. In recent years, studies by cancer experts have shown a significantly lower cancer rate for the Utah population than the U.S. in general. James E. Enstrom, UCLA epidemiologist, conducted a study on 10,000 nonsmokers and nondrinkers. "It illustrates a group of individuals [that] have healthy practice in regard to diet because of the large Mormon population. There is an absence among most of the population [and] alcohol is not consumed. These are factors that are often related to cancer risk."[13]

Because the body and the spirit are both so critical to the full development of the individual, members believe that spirituality is adversely affected by the consumption of harmful substances. In the revelation on the Word of Wisdom is found this promise: "All saints who remember to keep and do these sayings, walking in obedience to the commandments, shall receive health in their navel and marrow to their bones; and shall find wisdom and great treasures of knowledge, even hidden treasures; and shall run and not be weary, and shall walk and not faint. And I, the Lord, give unto them a promise, that the destroying angel shall pass by them, as the children of Israel, and not slay them." (D&C 89:18–21.)

GROWTH AND THE FUTURE

The LDS Church grew to become an established body of believers by the time of Joseph Smith's death and the exodus across the plains to the Great Basin. As missionary work has intensified, the number of converts has steadily grown to more than 300,000 per year at the time of this writing. As recently as the 1950s the Church was viewed as largely a Western American church; however, congregations are now found in Africa, Asia, the Philippines, Europe, the islands of the Pacific, and in large numbers in Central and South

---

[13] As reported in *The Journal of the National Cancer Institute*, December 1989.

America. Rodney Stark, a noted sociologist of religion, following a serious investigation of patterns of LDS growth, observed, "The Church of Jesus Christ of Latter-day Saints, the Mormons, will soon achieve a worldwide following comparable to that of Islam, Buddhism, Christianity, Hinduism, and the other dominant world faiths. . . . Indeed, today they stand on the threshold of becoming the first major faith to appear on earth since the Prophet Mohammed rode out of the desert." Stark then suggested that a 30-percent growth rate per decade will result in more than 60 million Latter-day Saints by the year 2080. A 50-percent-per-decade growth rate, which is actually lower than the rate each decade since World War II, will result in 265 million Mormons by 2080.[14]

What are the reasons for such growth? What attracts people generally to The Church of Jesus Christ of Latter-day Saints? First of all, many people, weary of moral decline and what they perceive to be an erosion of time-honored values, are drawn to a church and a people who seem to be, as one journalist put it, "a repository of old-fashioned values, an American success story."[15] The Latter-day Saints hold to absolute truths concerning God and man, and right and wrong. Second, the Latter-day Saint doctrines concerning God's plan for his children provide answers to such questions as where we came from, why we are here, and where we are going—and these answers appeal to large numbers of men and women who are searching for meaning in life and for answers to the perplexities of our existence. The focus on the family is seen as refreshing and, as we noted above, badly overdue in a world that seems to be drifting rapidly from its moorings.

One aspect of the doctrine of a divine plan—that which deals with heaven and the hereafter—is especially appealing

---

[14] "The Rise of a New World Faith," *Review of Religious Research,* vol. 26, no. 1, 1984, pp. 18–23.
[15] Peter Steinfels, "Despite Growth, Mormons Find New Hurdles," *New York Times,* September 15, 1991, sec. 1, p. 1.

to those who encounter the LDS Church. "Expressions of the eternal nature of love and the hope for heavenly reunion," Colleen McDannell and Bernhard Lang have written, "persist in contemporary Christianity."

Such sentiments, however, are not situated within a theological structure. Hoping to meet one's family after death is a wish and not a theological argument. While most Christian clergy would not deny that wish, contemporary theologians are not interested in articulating the motif of meeting again in theological terms. The motifs of the modern heaven—eternal progress, love, and fluidity between earth and the other world—while acknowledged by pastors in their funeral sermons, are not fundamental to contemporary Christianity. Priests and pastors might tell families that they will meet their loved ones in heaven as a means of consolation, but contemporary thought does not support that belief as it did in the nineteenth century. There is no longer a strong theological commitment.

The major exception to this caveat is the teaching of The Church of Jesus Christ of Latter-day Saints, whose members are frequently referred to as the Mormons. The modern perspective on heaven—emphasizing the nearness and similarity of the other world to our own and arguing for the eternal nature of love, family, progress, and work—finds its greatest proponent in Latter-day Saints' (LDS) understanding of the afterlife. While most contemporary Christian groups neglect afterlife beliefs, what happens to people after they die is crucial to LDS teachings and rituals. Heavenly theology is the result not of mere speculation, but of revelation given to past and present church leaders. . . .

. . . There has been . . . no alteration of the LDS understanding of the afterlife since its articulation by Joseph Smith. If anything, the Latter-day Saints in the twentieth century have become even bolder in their assertion of the importance of their heavenly theology. . . . In the light of what they perceive as a Christian world which has given up belief in heaven, many Latter-day Saints feel even more of a responsibility to define the meaning of death and eternal life.[16]

Though it may seem odd at first glance, there is another reason why the Church seems to be growing so rapidly—because of the requirements and the demands it makes upon its members. "Let us here observe," the early Saints were taught, "that a religion that does not require the sacrifice of all things never has power sufficient to produce the faith necessary unto life and salvation."[17] In other words, a religion that does not ask anything of its congregants can promise them little. Easy religion and convenient theology are not satisfying to the soul. People yearn for something to which they can commit themselves completely, something worthy of their devotion and their investment of time, talents, and means. It is worth noting, therefore, that recent studies in the sociology of religion indicate that the religious organizations that are growing the fastest are, ironically, those whose costs of membership—material, social, and spiritual—are greater. The greater the investment in terms of participation and involvement, the greater the sticking power and the attractiveness to the seeker of truth.[18]

A number of years ago an article appeared in *Christianity Today* entitled "Why Your Neighbor Joined the Mormon Church." Five reasons were given:

1. The Mormons show genuine love and concern by taking care of the needs of their people.

2. The Mormons strive to build the family unit.

3. The Mormons provide for their young people.

4. The Mormon church is a layman's church.

5. The Mormons believe that Divine Revelation is the basis for their practices.

---

[16] *Heaven: A History* (New Haven and London: Yale University Press, 1988), pp. 313, 322.

[17] *Lectures on Faith* 6:7.

[18] See Roger Finke and Rodney Stark, *The Churching of America, 1776–1990* (New Brunswick, New Jersey: Rutgers University Press, 1992), p. 255.

After a brief discussion of each of the above, the author of the article concluded, "In a day when many are hesitant to claim that God has said anything definitive, the Mormons stand out in contrast, and many people are ready to listen to what the Mormons think the voice of God says. It is tragic that their message is false, but it is nonetheless a lesson to us that people are many times ready to hear a voice of authority."[19]

Jesus taught of the importance of judging things—prophets, for example—by their fruits, by what comes of their ministry and teachings. (Matthew 7:15–20.) It is not the place of this book to argue for the truthfulness of The Church of Jesus Christ of Latter-day Saints; rather, this work is intended to inform, to build understanding. I say only that there must be some reason why large numbers of people are coming into the LDS Church. If the Lord is right, evil trees cannot bring forth good fruit. Something is working.

---

[19] *Christianity Today,* October 11, 1974, pp. 11–13.

C H A P T E R   1 3

THE END TIMES

Eschatology, or the study of "end times," is an important dimension of LDS life and theology. What the Latter-day Saints believe about the events to come significantly affects how they now live and conduct their affairs. Without a knowledge of what lies ahead, one cannot have the proper perspective of the overall plan of God to save his children. LDS scriptures are thus filled with references to the last days, to both great and dreadful things that lie ahead. A knowledge of the glories and the trials does much to motivate individuals and congregations to greater fidelity and devotion, to "hold on" to the iron rod, the word of God. The growing fascination in today's world with such phenomena as the Near Death Experience, angels, and miracles attest to our deepest desires to make sense out of what would otherwise be a chaotic existence, a yearning to know that there is a God, that there is life after death, that there is purpose to life's challenges and tragedies.

Latter-day Saints believe that God can and does speak to men and women through inspiration. They believe the Almighty can make his will known for the world through prophets, and that those prophets have the capacity not only to speak for the present but also to predict future occurrences. Mormons therefore accept wholeheartedly the predictive prophecies in the Old and New Testaments, as well as other prophetic oracles that have come subsequently through Joseph Smith and his successors. Prophet leaders have counseled the members of the Church to take a wholesome and sane approach to prophecy, to study and be aware of the prophetic word but to live each day with confidence and conviction that God is in his heavens and will bring to pass his purposes in process of time. Church leaders have therefore counseled against what might be called either eschatomania (an unhealthy obsession with signs of the times) or eschatophobia (an unhealthy fear of what lies ahead).[1]

THE SECOND COMING

Jesus came to earth as a mortal being in the meridian of time. He taught the gospel, bestowed divine authority, organized the Church, and suffered and died as an infinite atoning sacrifice for the sins of the world. He stated that he would come again, would return, not as the meek and lowly Nazarene but as the Lord of Sabaoth, the Lord of Hosts, the Lord of Armies. His second coming is thus spoken of as his coming "in glory," meaning in his true identity as the God of all creation, the Redeemer and Judge. His second coming is described as both *great* and *dreadful*—great for those who have been faithful and therefore look forward to his coming, and dreadful to those who have done despite to the spirit of grace and who therefore hope against hope that he will never return. The Second Coming in glory is in fact "the end of the world," meaning the end of worldliness, the destruction of the wicked. (Pearl of Great Price, Joseph Smith—Matthew 1:4, 31.) At this coming the righteous will be quickened and caught up to meet him, and the earth will be transformed from a fallen orb to a paradisiacal sphere. The wicked will be destroyed by the brightness of the Lord's coming; their spirits will take up a residence in the postmortal spirit world to await

---

[1] See Millard J. Erickson, *Christian Theology* (Grand Rapids, Mich.: Baker Book House, 1986), p. 1,152.

the last resurrection at the end of the thousand years. (Revelation 20:4–5; D&C 43:18; 63:17–18; 76:81–85; 88:100–101.) The Second Coming in glory will initiate the Millennial reign.

The scriptures speak of the Master returning as "a thief in the night." (1 Thessalonians 5:2; 2 Peter 3:10.) It is true that no mortal has known, does now know, or will yet know the precise day of the Lord's Second Advent. This is true for prophets and apostles as well as the rank and file of society and the Church. On the other hand, the people of God are promised that if they are in tune with the Spirit, they can discern the season. The Apostle Paul chose the descriptive analogy of a pregnant woman about to deliver. She may not know the exact hour or day when the birth is to take place, but one thing she knows for sure: it will be soon. It *must* be soon! The impressions and feelings and signs within her own body so testify. In that day, surely the members of the body of Christ will be pleading for the Lord to deliver the travailing earth, to bring an end to corruption and degradation, to introduce an era of peace and righteousness. And those who give heed to the words of scripture, and especially to the living oracles, will stand as the "children of light, and the children of the day," those who "are not of the night, nor of darkness." (1 Thessalonians 5:2–5.) In the Doctrine and Covenants is found this admonition: "The coming of the Lord draweth nigh, and *it overtaketh the world as a thief in the night*—therefore, gird up your loins, that you may be the children of light, and that day shall not overtake you as a thief." (D&C 106:4–5; emphasis added.)

When Christ comes in glory, all will know. "Be not deceived," the Master warned in a modern revelation, "but continue in steadfastness, looking forth for the heavens to be shaken, and the earth to tremble and to reel to and fro as a drunken man, and for the valleys to be exalted, and for the mountains to be made low, and for the rough places to become smooth." (D&C 49:23.) "Wherefore, prepare ye for the coming of the Bridegroom; go ye, go ye out to meet him. For behold, he shall stand upon the mount of Olivet, and upon the mighty ocean, even the great deep, and upon the islands of the sea, and upon the land of Zion. And he shall utter his voice out of Zion, and he shall speak from Jerusalem, and *his voice shall be heard among all people;* and it shall be a voice as the voice of many waters, and as the voice of a great thunder, which shall break down the mountains, and the valleys shall not be found." (D&C 133:19–22; emphasis added.)

The righteous dead from ages past—those who died true in the faith since the resurrection was initiated in Christ's day—will come with the Savior when he returns in glory. The Prophet Joseph altered a passage in Paul's first epistle to the Thessalonians as follows: "I would not have you to be ignorant, brethren, concerning them which are asleep, that ye sorrow not, even as others which have no hope. For if we believe that Jesus died and rose again, even so them also which sleep in Jesus will God bring with him. For this we say unto you by the word of the Lord, that they who are alive at the coming of the Lord, shall not prevent [precede] them who remain unto the coming of the Lord, who are asleep. For the Lord himself shall descend from heaven with a shout, with the voice of the archangel, and with the trump of God: and the dead in Christ shall rise first; then they who are alive, shall be caught up together into the clouds with them who remain, to meet the Lord in the air; and so shall we be ever with the Lord." (Joseph Smith Translation, 1 Thessalonians 4:13–17.)

Those who are of at least a terrestrial level of righteousness—good and noble men and women—will continue to live as mortals after the Lord returns. The faithful will live to "the age of man"—in the words of Isaiah, the age of one hundred (Isaiah 65:20)—and will then pass through death and be changed instantly from mortality to resurrected immortality. "Yea, and blessed are the dead that die in the Lord, . . . when the Lord shall come, and old things shall pass away, and all things become new, they shall rise from the dead and shall not die after, and shall receive an inheritance before the Lord, in the holy city. And he that liveth when the Lord shall come, and hath kept the faith, blessed is he; nevertheless, it is appointed to him to die at the age of man. Wherefore, children shall grow up until they become old"—that is, no longer shall little ones die before the time of accountability; "old men shall die; but they shall not sleep in the dust, but they shall be changed in the twinkling of an eye." (D&C 63:49–51; see also JST, Isaiah 65:20.)

Malachi prophesied that "the day cometh, that shall burn as an oven; and all the proud, yea, and all that do wickedly, shall be stubble: and the day that cometh shall burn them up, saith the Lord of hosts, that it shall leave them neither root nor branch." (Malachi 4:1; compare Book of Mormon, 2 Nephi 26:4; D&C 133:64.) The second coming of Christ in glory is a day wherein "every corruptible thing, both of man, or of the beasts of the field, or of the fowls of the heavens, or of the fish of the sea, that dwells upon all the face of the earth, shall be consumed; and also that of element shall melt with fervent heat; and all things shall become new, that my knowledge and glory may dwell upon all the earth." (D&C 101:24–25; compare 133:41; 2 Peter 3:10.) Joseph Fielding Smith wrote, "Somebody said, 'Brother Smith, do you mean to say that it is going to be literal fire?' I said, 'Oh, no, it will not be literal fire any more than it was literal water that covered the earth in the flood.'"[2]

THE MILLENNIUM

The doctrine of the Latter-day Saints is that the second coming in glory of Jesus Christ ushers in the Millennium. In a sense, the Latter-day Saints might be called premillennialists; the Millennium will not come because men and women on earth have become noble and good, because Christian charity will have spread across the globe and goodwill is the order of the day. The Millennium will not come because technological advances and medical miracles will have extended human life or because peace treaties among warring nations will have soothed injured feelings and eased political tensions. The

---

[2] *The Signs of the Times* (Salt Lake City: Deseret Book Co., 1942), p. 41.

Millennium will be brought in by power, by the power of him who is the King of kings and Lord of lords. Satan will be bound by power, and the glory of the Millennium will be maintained by the righteousness of those who are permitted to live on earth during that time. (Book of Mormon, 1 Nephi 22:15, 26.)

At the beginning of the Millennium, the earth and all things upon it will be quickened, made alive, and transfigured—lifted to a higher plane for a season. The earth will be transformed from a telestial to a terrestrial glory, to that paradisiacal condition that prevailed in Eden before the Fall. (Pearl of Great Price, Articles of Faith 1:10.) There will indeed be a new heaven and a new earth. (Isaiah 65:17; Revelation 21:1.) Further, as Orson Pratt, an early apostle, explained, "All the inhabitants who are spared from this fire [the fire accompanying the glory of Christ at his coming]—those who are not proud, and who do not do wickedly, will be cleansed more fully and filled with the glory of God. A partial change will be wrought upon them, not a change to immortality [which would come after their death and resurrection], . . . but so great will be the change then wrought that the children who are born into the world will grow up without sin unto salvation. Why will this be so? Because that fallen nature, introduced by the fall, and transferred from parents to children, from generation to generation, will be, in a measure, eradicated by this change."[3]

Latter-day Saints affirm that the "first resurrection" began with the resurrection of Christ. (See Matthew 27:52–53.) All of the prophets and those who gave heed to the words of the prophets, the faithful who lived from the days of Adam to the time of the rise of Jesus from the tomb, came forth with the Master from the dead. (Book of Mormon, Mosiah 15:21–22.) When the Redeemer returns in glory to take charge of affairs on earth, with him will come a host of the righteous dead, men and women who will possess physical, resurrected, immortal bodies. The first resurrection will thereby resume and continue for the period of one thousand years we know

---

[3] *Journal of Discourses* 16:319.

as the Millennium. Those who have died true to the faith, those who have lived from the time of Christ's resurrection to the time of his second coming, will come to earth to dwell with their Lord and God. Although men and women who are alive at the time of Christ's second coming will be changed and quickened, they will yet continue to live as mortals until, as we mentioned earlier, they arrive at the "age of man," at which time they will be "changed in the twinkling of an eye," changed instantaneously from mortality to resurrected immortality. (Isaiah 65:20; D&C 63:50–51.)

President Brigham Young stated, "If the Latter-day saints think, when the kingdom of God is established on the earth, that all the inhabitants of the earth will join the church called Latter-day Saints, they are egregiously mistaken. I presume there will be as many sects and parties then as now."[4] On another occasion he stated, "When Jesus comes to rule and reign King of Nations as he now does King of Saints, the veil of the covering will be taken from all nations, that all flesh may see his glory together, but that will not make them all Saints. Seeing the Lord does not make a man a Saint, seeing an Angel does not make a man a Saint by any means." Brother Brigham then added that the leaders of the nations in that day, "kings and potentates of the nations will come up to Zion to inquire after the ways of the Lord, and to seek out the great knowledge, wisdom, and understanding manifested through the Saints of the Most High. They will inform the people of God that they belong to such and such a Church, and do not wish to change their religion."[5] In short, "in the millennium men will have the privilege of being Presbyterians, Methodists or Infidels, but they will not have the privilege of treating the name and character of Deity as they have done heretofore. No, but every knee shall bow and every tongue confess to the glory of God the Father that Jesus is the Christ."[6]

---

[4] Ibid., 11:275.
[5] Ibid., 2:316.
[6] Ibid., 12:274.

The Millennium will be a life without physical pain, premature death, and in general the sorrow that accompanies sin and waywardness, as well as dishonesty and greed. Isaiah declared that in that day "the wolf also shall dwell with the lamb, and the leopard shall lie down with the kid; and the calf and the young lion and the fatling together; and a little child shall lead them. And the cow and the bear shall feed; their little ones shall lie down together: and the lion shall eat straw like the ox. And the sucking child shall play on the hole of the asp, and the weaned child shall put his hand on the cockatrice' den. They shall not hurt nor destroy in all my holy mountain." (Isaiah 11:6–9; compare 65:25.) As described in the Doctrine and Covenants, "in that day the enmity of man, and the enmity of beasts, yea, the enmity of all flesh"—an animosity, a natural tension and unrest that came as a result of the Fall—"shall cease from before [the Lord's] face." (D&C 101:26.)

Mortals will inhabit the earth, alongside immortals, during the entirety of the thousand years. Men and women who abide the day of the Lord's coming in glory will continue to live on the earth in an Edenic or paradisiacal state. They will labor and study and grow and interact and love and socialize as before, but such things will be undertaken in a totally moral environment. "When the Savior shall appear," Joseph Smith instructed the Latter-day Saints in 1843, "we shall see him as he is. We shall see that he is a man like ourselves. And that same sociality that exists among us here will exist among us there, only it will be coupled with eternal glory, which glory we do not now enjoy." (D&C 130:1–2.) Thus, for the Latter-day Saints, eternal life or salvation consists of two things: (1) being fully sanctified and empowered by God, and (2) continuing with the family unit into eternity. (D&C 132:19–20.) The relationships that result in the deepest and most profound love in this life—family relationships—are intended to be eternal.

Isaiah prophesied that people in the Millennium will "build houses, and inhabit them; and they shall plant vineyards, and eat the fruit of them. They shall not build, and another inhabit; they shall not plant, and another eat." (Isaiah 65:21–22.) That is to say, in the Millennium men and women will enjoy the fruits of their labors. In a world where there is no extortion, no bribery, no organized crime, where there are no unjust laws, no class distinctions of men and women according to income or chances for learning, people will no longer be preyed upon by the perverse or the malicious or forced to relocate because of financial demands or pressures. Our longings for stability, longevity, and permanence will be largely satisfied, for Satan and those who have spread his influence will have no place on the earth during this glorious era. For a thousand years men and women will live lives of quiet nobility, will bow the knee and acknowledge Jesus the Messiah as the King of Zion and the Redeemer of all humankind.

Latter-day Saints teach, in harmony with the Bible (see Revelation 20:1–8), that there will come a time at the end of the thousand years when "men again begin to deny their God." (D&C 29:22.) Some will choose, despite the light and truth that surround them, to come out in open rebellion against God the Father, his Beloved Son, and the plan of salvation. Satan will be loosed again "for a little season" that he might "gather together his armies." (D&C 88:111; see also 43:31.) "Michael, the seventh angel, even the archangel, shall gather together his armies, even the hosts of heaven. And the devil shall gather together his armies; even the hosts of hell, and shall come up to battle against Michael and his armies. And then cometh the battle of the great God"—known as the Battle of Gog and Magog—"and the devil and his armies shall be cast away into their own place, and they shall not have power over the saints any more at all." (D&C 88:112–14.) At the end of the thousand years those who will receive a telestial glory will come forth in the resurrection, as will the sons of perdition. (D&C 76:38–39; 88:15–32, 102.)

After the Battle of Gog and Magog, we come to that time known to the Latter-day Saints as the "end of the earth" (D&C 88:101; Pearl of Great Price, Joseph Smith—Matthew 1:55), the final cleansing and celestialization of the planet.

The earth will then be a fit abode for the true and faithful, "that bodies who are of the celestial kingdom may possess it forever and ever; for, for this intent was it made and created, and for this intent are they [the Saints of God] sanctified." (D&C 88:20.) The Day of Judgment follows the last resurrection. Inasmuch as the Father has committed all judgment to the Son (John 5:22), Christ, who is the "Holy One of Israel," the "keeper of the gate" (Book of Mormon, 2 Nephi 9:41), will pronounce the final judgment upon all men and women, righteous and wicked. The children of God will then be assigned forevermore to their respective kingdoms of glory— celestial, terrestrial, and telestial. The sons of perdition will likewise be assigned to outer darkness or eternal hell, to a kingdom of no glory. (D&C 88:24.)

Unlike so many in the religious world, the Latter-day Saints anticipate celestial life on a material world. Orson Pratt eloquently made the point as follows: "A Saint who is one in deed and truth, does not look for an immaterial heaven, but he expects a heaven with lands, houses, cities, vegetation, rivers, and animals; with thrones, temples, palaces, kings, princes, priests, and angels; with food, raiment, musical instruments, etc., all of which are material. Indeed, the Saints' eternal home is a redeemed, glorified, celestial material creation, inhabited by glorified material beings, male and female, organized into families, embracing all the relationships of husbands and wives, parents and children, where sorrow, crying, pain, and death will be known no more." On this earth, Elder Pratt continued, the Saints of God "expect to live, with body, parts, and holy passions; on it they expect to move and have their being." In short, "materiality is indelibly stamped upon the very heaven of heavens, upon all the eternal creations; it is the very essence of all existence."[7]

---

[7] *Masterful Discourses and Writings of Orson Pratt* (Salt Lake City: Bookcraft, 1962), pp. 62–63.

CHAPTER   14

QUESTIONS

AND ANSWERS

There are obvious limitations upon what can be said in a book of this type. An introduction can do no more than leave an impression or two and encourage the interested reader to pursue the subject in more detail at leisure. Because we simply cannot cover all the bases, and because there may be matters that are still unresolved in the minds of readers, I have felt the need to pose and then respond to what I believe to be some of the most frequently asked questions. Although some of these issues may have been explained or touched upon in the preceding chapters, this chapter is written so as to be read independent of the rest of the work.

1. *The Mormons are obviously not Catholic. Are they Protestant?*

The Church of Jesus Christ of Latter-day Saints did not break away from Roman Catholicism and thus is not a Protestant church. Latter-day Saints claim to be a restoration of primitive Christianity, of the church Jesus established in the first century. They believe that with the deaths of the apostles came also a loss of divine authority as well as a loss of plain and precious doctrinal truths. They feel that God chose to begin a restoration of that authority and those truths when he called Joseph Smith in the spring of 1820. Thus it might be appropriate to speak of the LDS Church as neither a Catholic church nor a Protestant church but rather as a *restored* church.

2. *Much has been said about the Mormons not being Christian. Are they?*

In recent years the criticism of Latter-day Saints and a movement to exclude them from the category of *Christian* have intensified. There are those who feel uncomfortable with them because of their belief in modern prophets and additional scripture. Others reject the LDS claim to Christianity because the Church does not subscribe to the creeds of Christendom or is not in the historical Christian tradition. On what basis, then, do the Latter-day Saints themselves claim to be Christian? They believe in Jesus Christ; that he is the Son of the Eternal Father, the Only Begotten in the flesh; that Christ is God, that he is Lord and Savior, the Redeemer of the world; that we are saved by obedience to his commandments and by virtue of his atoning blood; that only through reliance upon his merits, mercy, and grace can people find happiness here and eternal reward hereafter; and that his was the only perfect and sinless life, a life to be emulated and followed. Jesus Christ is the central figure in the doctrine and practice of The Church of Jesus Christ of Latter-day Saints. That so many misunderstand, prejudge, and exclude is sad and strangely ironic.

3. *Do the Latter-day Saints worship Joseph Smith? What is the relationship of Joseph Smith to subsequent Church presidents?*

The Latter-day Saints worship God the Father and his Son Jesus Christ. These members of the Godhead are divine, immortal, and glorified beings. The Latter-day Saints revere Joseph Smith as a modern prophet, as a covenant spokesman, as a mouthpiece for Deity in the same sense that Abraham, Moses, Isaiah, and Jeremiah were. Joseph Smith was a mortal man. The Mormons do not worship Joseph Smith. They value his words, study his sermons and writings (along with scriptural teachings found in the Bible), and treasure his legacy. Joseph Smith claimed to be no more than a servant in the hands of God, and Latter-day Saints do not afford him more honor and devotion than is appropriate.

The Latter-day Saints believe that all of the presidents of the Church who have succeeded Joseph Smith (see appendix 3) have held the same divine calling, the same rights and priesthood authority, and have been entitled to the designation of prophet, seer, and revelator to the Church. Joseph Smith is in a significant position in the sense that he is what is called a *dispensation head*, a man called to restore the knowledge of God, of Christ, and of the plan of salvation following a period of apostasy. The dispensation head, a prophet's prophet, establishes those doctrines and authorities once again on earth, and those who follow him, though prophets in their own right, stand as echoes and affirmations of his original testimony to the world, and they also seek for and declare new revelation as it comes.

4. *How do Mormons feel about other churches? Is not their claim to being the "only true church" exclusivistic and even unchristian?*

Latter-day Saints believe that truth is to be found throughout the earth—among men and women in all walks of life, among sages and philosophers, and among people of differing religious persuasions. But they do claim that through the call of Joseph Smith and his successors, and through the establishment of The Church of Jesus Christ of Latter-day Saints, the *fullness* of the gospel of Jesus Christ has been restored to earth. They value the truths had among the children of God everywhere but believe that theirs is the "only true church" in the sense that the same divine authority and the same doctrines of salvation had from the beginning are now to be found *in their fullness* in the LDS faith. It is odd that Protestant Christianity should be so offended with Joseph Smith's statement that 19th-century Christianity was off course; is that not exactly what those protesters like Luther, Calvin, and Zwingli said in regard to the Roman Catholic Church?

5. *Doesn't the Bible warn about those who seek to add to or take away from the scriptures? How can the Latter-day Saints then justify*

having additional books of scripture? Does this not disqualify them as Christians?

First of all, it appears that the passages in the Old Testament that warn against such things (Deuteronomy 4:2; 12:32) are actually warning against adding to the books of Moses, the Pentateuch. This certainly could not have reference to adding to the Old Testament in general, or else we could not in good conscience accept the thirty-four books that follow the Pentateuch. Furthermore, the warning attached to the end of the Revelation of John is a warning against adding to or taking away from "the words of the prophecy of this book" (Revelation 22:18), namely, the Apocalypse. Most important, Latter-day Saints believe that these warnings have to do with the condemnation associated with a man, an uninspired man, a man not called of God, taking upon himself the responsibility to add to or take from the canon of scripture. But it is God's right to speak beyond what he has spoken already (as he certainly did in the person and messages and works of Jesus himself), and Latter-day Saints feel that God should be allowed to direct and empower his children as need arises. It is not for us to set up bounds and stakes for the Almighty. Nowhere in the Bible itself do we learn that God will no longer speak directly to his children or add to past scripture.

6. *Isn't it enough to be a good person? Why must one belong to a certain church in order to be saved?*

It is important to be a good person, a moral person, a person of integrity. The gospel is intended, however, to do more than make us good. The gospel is the power of God unto salvation (Romans 1:16), the power to transform good people into Christlike people, noble souls into holy souls. The church is the custodian of the gospel—the divine authority and the truths of salvation—and so Latter-day Saints do not believe that one can come unto Christ independent of (or in opposition to) the Church of Jesus Christ. They believe there is "one Lord, one faith, one baptism" (Ephesians 4:5), and that the sacraments or ordinances of salvation, administered by the priesthood held in the Church, are prerequisite to entrance into the kingdom of God.

7. *What is the difference between The Church of Jesus Christ of Latter-day Saints (Salt Lake City, Utah) and the Reorganized Church of Jesus Christ of Latter Day Saints (Independence, Missouri)?*

After the death of Joseph Smith, Jr., there was a question in the minds of many as to who should lead the Church. One branch of the Saints felt that Joseph had given strict instructions to the effect that at his death the First Presidency would be dissolved, and the Quorum of the Twelve Apostles, then under Brigham Young's direction, would be responsible for leading the people. Another group believed that Joseph the Prophet had ordained his eldest son to succeed him. The former group were led by Brigham Young from Nauvoo, Illinois in 1846 and traveled across the plains to Salt Lake City, Utah. This group, sometimes called the "Utah Mormons," was The Church of Jesus Christ of Latter-day Saints. In 1860 the second group formally organized themselves with Joseph Smith III as their leader. Their headquarters moved from Plano, Illinois, to Lamoni, Iowa, and finally to Independence, Missouri. This was the Reorganized Church of Jesus Christ of Latter Day Saints (RLDS). The first major division, therefore, between the two churches was over the question of succession—apostolic or patriarchal. Since 1860 the LDS and RLDS churches have divided over several matters of doctrine and practice.

8. *Don't the Latter-day Saints basically believe in a different Jesus?*

The Latter-day Saints believe in Jesus of Nazareth, the same who came into the world during the years that such leaders as Herod and Pontius Pilate and Caiaphas were in power. They believe in the testimonies of the New Testament writers concerning our Lord's divine Sonship and his miraculous doings. It is true that they accept additional books of scripture that reveal additional things about the life and ministry of Jesus, but it could hardly be said that they worship a different Savior.

9. *Why are there no crosses in LDS churches? Is it true that the Latter-day Saints do not believe Jesus died on the cross for our sins?*

Latter-day Saints believe the Atonement of Jesus Christ to be the central act of all history, just as Christians around the world do. According to LDS teachings, Jesus' suffering in the garden was not just the awful anticipation of the cross. Instead, the atoning sacrifice was performed in the Garden of Gethsemane and on the cross. That is, the suffering that began in Gethsemane was completed on Golgotha the next day. Thus for LDS people the acceptance of the Atonement is not symbolized by the cross, whether on or in buildings, on religious vestments, or on church literature. In addition, Gordon B. Hinckley, fourteenth president of the Church, observed that "the cross is the symbol of the dying Christ, while our message is a declaration of the living Christ." He noted further that "the lives of our people must become the only meaningful expression of our faith and in fact, therefore, the symbol of our worship."[1]

10. *Don't the Mormons believe they will be saved by their works and not by the grace of Christ?*

Entrance into God's kingdom comes through covenant—a two-way promise between God and man. The follower of Christ promises to do what he can do—have faith, repent, be baptized, receive the Holy Ghost, endure faithfully to the end, and undertake deeds of Christian service. God on his part agrees to do for us what we could not do for ourselves—forgive our sins, transform our souls and purify our hearts, resurrect us from the dead, and save us hereafter in a kingdom of glory. LDS scriptures are very clear and consistent in stating that salvation or eternal life is a gift, in fact, the greatest of all the gifts of God. (D&C 6:13; 14:7.) Salvation is not something that can be purchased, bartered for, or, in the strictest sense, earned. Over and over again, the Book of Mormon, for example, affirms that men and women are saved by the grace of Jesus Christ and that there is no other way whereby salvation can be acquired. (2 Nephi 10:24; 25:23; Alma 22:14.) On the

---

[1] *Be Thou an Example* (Salt Lake City: Deseret Book Co., 1981), pp. 85–86.

other hand, good works are expected of those who claim to have taken upon them the name of Christ. In fact, it is only as they strive to do their best to keep their part of the Christian covenant that the grace or divine enabling power can be extended and received as the free gift that it is. (Moroni 10:32.) In short, good works are necessary but not sufficient for salvation. The theological issue is thus not whether people are saved by grace or by works. Instead, the greater questions are: In whom do I trust? Upon whom do I rely? The Book of Mormon prophets attest that the people of God must always rely wholly (alone) upon the merits and mercy of the Holy Messiah. (1 Nephi 10:6; 2 Nephi 31:19; Moroni 6:4.)

11. *If God was once a man, as Latter-day Saints believe, how can he be "from eternity to eternity?"*

Joseph Smith did in fact teach that God is a Man of Holiness, an exalted and glorified man. Latter-day Saints really do not claim to know much beyond that, except that over a long period of time our Heavenly Father gained the knowledge, power, and divine attributes he now possesses; there is no knowledge of which he is ignorant and no power he does not possess. Because he has held his exalted status for a longer period than any of us can conceive, he is able to speak in terms of eternity and can state that he is from everlasting to everlasting. One Church leader, Joseph Fielding Smith, explained, "From eternity to eternity means from the spirit existence through the probation which we are in, and then back again to the eternal existence which will follow. Surely this is everlasting, for when we receive the resurrection, we will never die. We all existed in the first eternity. I think I can say of myself and others, we are from eternity; and we will be to eternity everlasting, if we receive the exaltation."[2]

12. *If God has a body, as the Mormons teach, is he not then limited in some way? For example, if he has a body, he surely cannot be in more than one place at a time.*

---

[2] *Doctrines of Salvation*, 3 vols., comp. Bruce R. McConkie (Salt Lake City: Bookcraft, 1954–56), 1:12; see also Bruce R. McConkie, *The Promised Messiah* (Salt Lake City: Deseret Book Co., 1978), p. 166.

For the Latter-day Saints, God is not just a force in the universe, a spirit essence. He is a person, a glorified personage, a being with body, parts, and passions. He is the Father of our spirits and thus has tender regard for all of his children. He is approachable, knowable, and, like Jesus, can be touched by the feeling of our infirmities. (Hebrews 4:15.) In his corporeal or physical nature, he can be in only one place at a time. His divine nature is such, however, that his glory, his power, and his influence, meaning his Holy Spirit, fills the immensity of space and is the means by which he is omnipresent and by which law and light and life exist. (D&C 88:6–13.)

13. *Why are not such teachings found in the Book of Mormon? If the Book of Mormon is so fundamental to the faith of the Latter-day Saints, why does it not mention such things about Deity?*

Joseph Smith stated that the Book of Mormon is the keystone of the religion of the Latter-day Saints.[3] It teaches the gospel or doctrine of Christ as repetitively and clearly as any other scriptural work—that salvation is in Christ, and that men and women may come unto Christ through faith, repentance, baptism, and the receipt of the Holy Ghost. (2 Nephi 31; 3 Nephi 27.) These principles weave their way through the narrative for most of the 531 pages. As a fundamental scriptural record, the Book of Mormon sets forth the fundamental doctrines of salvation, namely, what people must do to be saved. Its writers do not concern themselves with many other doctrinal matters that are taught, for example, in the Doctrine and Covenants. The Book of Mormon does not treat directly such items as degrees of glory in the hereafter, eternal marriage, or the corporeal nature of God. The Book of Mormon contains the fullness of the gospel—the glad tidings concerning Jesus Christ—not the fullness of gospel doctrine. In a similar vein, most Christians are not troubled by the fact that the epistles of Paul contain many doctrinal matters that are not even mentioned by Jesus and the apostles in the four Gospels.

---

[3] *Teachings*, p. 194.

14. *Doesn't the Book of Mormon teach that there is only one God and that he is a spirit? Is this not a contradiction of other LDS teachings?*

Though the Book of Mormon prophet writers did speak of both the Father and the Son and of Jesus as the Son of God (see, for example, 1 Nephi 10:4, 17; 11:7, 24; 2 Nephi 25:16; Jacob 4:5, 11; Mosiah 3:8; Alma 5:50; Helaman 14:2; 3 Nephi 11:7; Mormon 5:14; Ether 12:18), there is no question but that Jesus Christ is the central character of the book. He is the Eternal God, the Lord Omnipotent, the Holy One of Israel. As far as salvation is concerned, there is only one God, and that being is Jesus Christ. That is to say, Jesus is both God and Son of God. (2 Nephi 11:7; Alma 11:26–33.) God is called a spirit in the Book of Mormon (Alma 18:18–30) because almost always the God being referred to is Jehovah, the spirit being who would come to earth and take a body as Jesus of Nazareth. There is no contradiction here, only a supreme emphasis upon Christ in the Book of Mormon.

15. *Isn't it true that Latter-day Saints are not concerned with salvation, only with what they call exaltation? Do they believe people must be "born again?"*

Latter-day Saints *are* concerned with salvation, with salvation from sin and death and hell, just like all other believing Christians. In scripture, especially LDS scripture, with but few exceptions (for example, in D&C 76:88; 132:17), when the word *salvation* or *saved* is used, eternal life or exaltation is meant. That is, almost always salvation is the same thing as exaltation, which is the same thing as eternal life, the highest of eternal rewards hereafter.

Latter-day Saints do believe that men and women must be born again to be saved. That is, "in addition to the physical ordinance of baptism and the laying on of hands, one must be spiritually born again to gain exaltation and eternal life."[4] In the words of another Church leader, "Mere compliance with the formality of the ordinance of baptism does not mean that

---

[4] Ezra Taft Benson, *A Witness and a Warning* (Salt Lake City: Deseret Book Co., 1988), p. 62.

a person has been born again. . . . The new birth takes place only for those who actually enjoy the gift or companionship of the Holy Ghost, only for those who are fully converted, who have given themselves without restraint to the Lord."[5]

16. *One of the problem areas for most people who begin to learn about the Latter-day Saints is the matter of polygamy in the history of the Church. How do they justify the practice?*

Joseph Smith claims to have first learned of the principle of the plurality of wives while translating the Bible in 1831. He had asked the Lord why such notable ancients as Abraham and Jacob had been permitted more than one wife and yet had seemingly maintained their righteous standing before God. With the answer to Joseph's query came the understanding that eventually the Latter-day Saints would be required to live this ancient law as a part of the "restoration of all things." (D&C 27:6; 86:10.)

This was not something the Prophet and others of the Church leadership wanted to do; there is sufficient historical evidence that Joseph procrastinated the teaching of the principle to the generality of the Church for many years, until, according to several sources, he was instructed that if he did not do so he would be punished by God. Plural marriage must be viewed as a *theological* principle the Latter-day Saints kept until almost the beginning of the twentieth century; neither the persistence nor the zeal of the Latter-day Saints in maintaining its practice can be grasped if it is seen as a social experiment or even as a sexual aberration. When the government of the United States officially declared the practice of polygamy to be unlawful, the leadership of the Church, in harmony with the Saints' belief in sustaining and upholding the law of the land (Pearl of Great Price, Articles of Faith 1:12), and acting under what they believed to be divine authority, announced the cessation of the practice in 1890.

17. *The twentieth-century LDS Church is very different from the nineteenth-century church. Many things have changed. How can the*

---

[5] Bruce R. McConkie, *Mormon Doctrine*, p. 101.

Mormons claim to possess eternal truth when things change as they have?

The Doctrine and Covenants speaks of the Church as both *true* and *living*. (D&C 1:30.) It is not, as someone has suggested, a fossilized faith but rather a kinetic kingdom. The Latter-day Saints believe that change is a part of growth and development, a vital sign that God continues to reveal his mind and will to his people. Joseph Smith taught, "This is the principle on which the government of heaven is conducted— by revelation adapted to the circumstances in which the children of the kingdom are placed."[6]

18. *Don't the "secret ceremonies" that go on in LDS temples make their faith more of a cult than a Christian church?*

The derisive label of *cult* frightens people and basically turns them off. It conjures up images of the bizarre, the unnatural, and even the demonic. The fact is, the first three definitions of cult in *Webster's Third International Dictionary* make no distinction between religion and cult. The fourth definition is the one, I suppose, most anti-Mormons have in mind: an unorthodox or spurious sect. One Evangelical scholar described cults as follows: (1) they are started by strong and dynamic leaders; (2) they believe in additional scripture; (3) they have rigid standards for membership; (4) they proselyte new converts; (5) the leaders or officials of the cult are not professional clergymen; (6) they believe in ongoing and continual communication from God; and (7) they claim some truth not available to other individuals or groups. By these standards of measure, the Latter-day Saints would certainly qualify as a cult. The problem, of course, is that the New Testament Christian Church would qualify also!

The ordinances of the temple are sacred, not secret. There are prerequisites to receiving them: faith, repentance, baptism, confirmation, and good standing in the Church. Any person who desires to go into the temple may prepare himself or herself to do so. The temple is open to all who are willing to comply with the prerequisites. A perusal of the New

---

[6] *Teachings*, p. 256.

Testament is all that is necessary to see that Jesus believed in the system of gospel prerequisites, that some things were to precede others. Many of his parables were delivered in order to veil meaning, to present messages of truth only to those who were prepared to receive them. (Matthew 13:10–13.) He taught that some sacred things are not to be casually distributed to the masses. (Matthew 7:6.) Of some matters the apostles were strictly warned, "Tell the vision to no man, until the Son of man be risen again from the dead." (Matthew 17:9.) The Latter-day Saints do not speak openly of the things taught in temples, but not to make the experience more mysterious or to heighten people's curiosity. Nor are temple ceremonies something the Latter-day Saints try to limit to a certain number of people; they urge every soul to qualify and prepare for the temple experience.

19. *Jesus taught that in the resurrection men and women "neither marry, nor are given in marriage." How do the Latter-day Saints reconcile this with their doctrine of eternal marriage?*

As was pointed out in chapters 7 and 8, The Church of Jesus Christ of Latter-day Saints claims to be the custodians of that priesthood power that binds and seals husbands and wives, parents and children, together for eternity. The Latter-day Saints believe that their Church administers the gospel of Jesus Christ, and that the gospel is everlasting in the sense that it was had in its fullness at various times by the ancients. They believe, for example, that eternal marriage was entered into by Adam and Eve, Abraham and Sarah, Isaac and Rebekah, Moses and Zipporah, and other men and women among the patriarchs, prophets, and worthy Former-day Saints. The power that Jesus gave to Peter, James, and John was the power to bind on earth and have those ordinances, including marriage, sealed everlastingly in the heavens. (Matthew 16:19; 18:18.)

Thus the incident that appears in Matthew 22 and Luke 20 in which Jesus states that "in the resurrection they neither marry, nor are given in marriage" would be explained by the Latter-day Saints as follows. To properly understand the scriptural text, we need only ask the standard question in interpretation: To whom is the message directed? The answer is the Sadducees, a Jewish religious sect that rejected Christ, his gospel, his priesthood, and even the doctrine of resurrection. In broader terms, the text applies to all others who reject the gospel of Jesus Christ or his saving and sealing powers. None such have any claim upon a sealing bond between marriage partners or in the family unit. The modern equivalent would be for a woman who does not believe in Christ, in his redemptive mission, or in resurrection, to ask a modern prophet which of the seven men to whom she had been married will be her husband in the world to come. The answer, obviously, is none of them. Because one unbeliever has been told that she has no claim on spouse or family in the world to come certainly is not to say that those who prove worthy of the full blessings of the Lord, including the blessings of eternal marriage, have no such promise. Thus the Doctrine and Covenants specifies that those who neither marry nor are given in marriage in the hereafter are those whose marriages are not performed by the sealing authority of the priesthood. (D&C 132:15–18.)

20. *Do the Mormons really believe that men and women can become gods? Are they then polytheists?*

Latter-day Saints believe that we come to the earth to take a physical body, to be schooled and trained and gain experiences here that we could not have in the premortal life, and then to seek to grow in faith and spiritual graces until we can qualify to go where God and Christ are. But they believe that eternal life consists in more than being *with* God; it entails being *like* God. A study of the Christian church reveals that the doctrine of the deification of man was taught at least into the fifth century by such notables as Irenaeus, Clement of Alexandria, Justin Martyr, Athanasius, and Augustine. Latter-day Saints would probably not agree with most of what was taught about deification by the early Christian church leaders, because they believe that many of the plain and precious truths concerning God and man had been lost by then. But I mention this to illustrate that the idea was not foreign to the people of the early church; the names mentioned were not pagan or Gnostic spokesmen but Christian.

The Latter-day Saint belief in man becoming as God is not dependent upon the early Christian concept, or upon such popular modern Christian thinkers as C. S. Lewis, who taught this notion.[7] In the vision of the hereafter given to Joseph Smith, described in chapter 5, is found this description of those who attain the highest or celestial glory: "Wherefore, as it is written, they are gods, even the sons of God." (D&C 76:58.) Godhood comes through the receipt of eternal life. Eternal life consists of two things: (1) the continuation of the family unit in eternity; and (2) inheriting, receiving, and being endowed with the fullness of the spirit and power of the Father. (D&C 132:19–20.) Latter-day Saints do not believe they will ever, worlds without end, unseat or oust God the Father or Jesus Christ. Those holy beings are and forever will be the Gods men and women worship. Men and women, like Christ, are made in the image and likeness of God; it is not robbery to be equal with God (Philippians 2:6), and like any father, our Heavenly Father wants his children to become and be all that he is. Spiritual growth to this lofty plain is not something that comes merely through hard work, though men and women are expected to do their best to keep their covenantal obligations. Deification is accomplished finally through the grace and goodness of Jesus Christ, who seeks that all of us might become joint heirs, co-inheritors with him, to all the Father has. (Romans 8:14–18.)

The Latter-day Saints, who believe in the Godhead, are no more polytheistic than are Christians who believe in the Trinity. God and Christ are the objects of our worship. Even though Mormons believe in the ultimate deification of man, I am unaware of any reference in LDS literature that speaks of worshiping any being other than the ones within the Godhead. Latter-day Saints believe in "one God" in the sense that

---

[7] See *The Weight of Glory and Other Addresses* (New York: Macmillan-Collier, 1960), p. 18; *Mere Christianity,* pp. 153–54, 174–75.

they love and serve one Godhead, one divine presidency, each of whom possesses all of the attributes of Godhood.

21. *Much has been said of discrimination against African American males and LDS women in regard to holding the priesthood in the LDS Church. Could you discuss this?*

Acting under what he and his people believed to be divine direction, some time late in the 1830s the Prophet Joseph Smith established a position that the blessings of the priesthood should be withheld from black members of The Church of Jesus Christ of Latter-day Saints. This practice continued in the Church through Joseph Smith's successors until the announcement of a revelation received by Spencer W. Kimball, twelfth president of the Church, in June of 1978. There is no statement directly from Joseph Smith himself offering commentary or doctrinal explanation for such an action, though the scriptural basis for a lineage-based granting or denial of priesthood may be found in the Pearl of Great Price. (Moses 7:8, 22; Abraham 1:21–27; see also Genesis 4:1–15; Moses 5:18–41.) Leaders of the Church have repeatedly affirmed that the position of the Church in regard to who does and does not bear the priesthood is a matter of revelation from heaven and not simply social or political expediency.

As to the fact that certain individuals or groups of people have not always had access to the full blessings of the gospel or the priesthood, there is also scriptural precedent. From the days of Moses to the coming of Jesus Christ, the Aaronic or Levitical Priesthood was conferred only upon worthy descendants of the tribe of Levi. In the first Christian century, the message of salvation was presented first to the Jews (the "lost sheep of the house of Israel," Matthew 10:5–6; 15:24) and then later, primarily through the labors of the Apostle Paul, to the Gentile nations. Ultimately the blessings of the Lord are for all people, "black and white, bond and free, male and female; and he remembereth the heathen; and all are alike unto God, both Jew and Gentile." (Book of Mormon, 2 Nephi 26:33.) At the same time, God has a plan, a divine timetable by which his purposes are brought to pass in and through his children on earth. He knows the end from the beginning and the times before appointed for specific doings and eventualities. (See Acts 17:26.) That timetable may not be ignored, slighted, or altered by finite man. The faithful seek to live in harmony with God's will and go forward in life with all patience and faith.

Women in the LDS Church are not ordained to the priesthood. The leaders of the Church have instructed that men and women have roles in life that are equally important but different. Some roles are best suited to the masculine nature, while women have natural and innate capacities to do some things that are more difficult for men. Because of the sanctity of the family and the home and because of the vital nature of the family in the preservation of society, Latter-day Saints teach that motherhood is the highest and holiest calling a woman can assume. The Mormons believe that women should search, study, learn, prepare, and develop in every way possible—socially, intellectually, and spiritually—but that no role in society will bring as much fulfillment or contribute more to the good of humankind than motherhood.

There is nothing in LDS doctrine to suggest that to be a man is preferred in the sight of God, or that the Almighty loves males more than females. Latter-day Saint theology condemns unrighteous dominion in any form, as well as any type of discrimination because of race, color, or gender. God is no respecter of persons. Women are the daughters of God, are entitled to every spiritual gift, every virtue, and every fruit of the Spirit. Priesthood is not maleness, nor should it be equated with male administration. A man who holds the priesthood does not have any advantage over a woman in qualifying for salvation in the highest heaven. Priesthood is divine authority given to worthy men, as a part of God's great plan of happiness. Why it is bestowed upon men and not women is not known. The highest ordinance of the priesthood, received in the temple, is given only to a man and a woman together.

A Latter-day Saint apostle, James E. Talmage, stated, "In the restored Church of Jesus Christ, the Holy Priesthood is conferred, as an individual bestowal, upon men only, and this in accordance with Divine requirement. It is not given to woman to exercise the authority of the Priesthood independently; nevertheless, in the sacred endowments associated with the ordinances pertaining to the House of the Lord, woman shares with man the blessings of the Priesthood. When the frailties and imperfections of mortality are left behind, in the glorified state of the blessed hereafter, husband and wife will administer in their respective stations, seeing and understanding alike, and co-operating to the full in the government of their family kingdom. Then shall woman be recompensed in rich measure for all the injustice that womanhood has endured in mortality. Then shall woman reign by Divine right, a queen in the resplendent realm of her glorified state, even as exalted man shall stand, priest and king unto the Most High God. Mortal eye cannot see nor mind comprehend the beauty, glory, and majesty of a righteous woman made perfect in the celestial kingdom of God."[8]

22. *Could you comment on the financial strength of the LDS Church?*

As pointed out in the last chapter, the LDS Church is growing. The number of members increases dramatically by the decade. Chapels, church buildings, and temples are under construction throughout the earth. It is true that the Church has substantial assets that accompany a growing organization. These assets are almost exclusively in its buildings—chapels, temples, seminary and institute of religion buildings, colleges and universities, welfare projects, mission homes, mission training centers, and family history (genealogy) facilities. All of these are money-consuming rather than money-producing assets. They do much to promote the work of the Church but are very expensive to maintain. There are a few income-producing business holdings, but these could not sustain the Church for very long. The Church is kept afloat through the

---

[8] James E. Talmage, "The Eternity of Sex," *Young Woman's Journal* 25 (October 1914), 602–3.

tithes and generous offerings of the members throughout the earth. Tithing is the Church's system of finance.

23. *Critics of the LDS Church have suggested that there are two types of Mormonism—the public (respected) version and the private (suspect) version.*

I will answer this one in a rather personal way. I have been a Latter-day Saint all my life. I was raised as a Latter-day Saint in Louisiana, and most of my friends were Roman Catholic or Protestant (Southern Baptist or Methodist). I spent my first eighteen years in Louisiana. I have since lived in New York, New Jersey, Massachusetts, Connecticut, Idaho, Florida, Georgia, and Utah, and I have been intimately involved in the work of the Church through the years. Since 1973 I have been employed by the LDS Church as a marriage and family counselor, seminary and institute of religion instructor, and dean of Religious Education and professor of Ancient Scripture at Brigham Young University. I have seen the Church from all sides—from right to left, and from top to bottom. I have worked closely with rank-and-file members and with Church leaders at all levels of administration. In all that time I have never encountered but one brand of Mormonism—the public version. I'm not sure where the secret brand—the one advertised by our critics as scheming, mischievous, power hungry, occultish, and dark—is to be found, but I haven't come across it. The reader would do well to be discerning and discriminating when it comes to some of the rather exotic assaults upon the LDS Church by its critics.

24. *Why do the Latter-day Saints send their missionaries out into the world, especially into Christian nations?*

Before The Church of Jesus Christ of Latter-day Saints was even organized, a spirit of enthusiasm and zeal was evident among those who encountered the message of Joseph Smith, the Book of Mormon, and the idea that God had chosen to restore truths and authorities to earth. That spirit intensified after the formal organization of the Church. Many of the revelations recorded in the Doctrine and Covenants instruct the Latter-day Saints to travel, to preach, and to proselyte. The Saints are told to proclaim the message of the

Restoration before individuals and congregations, in churches and in synagogues. Because they believe what they have to share with others represents a *fullness* of the gospel of Jesus Christ, and that the fullness is not found elsewhere, they feel a responsibility to make the message available to all who will hear. The commission given to the apostles when Jesus ascended into heaven, a commission to make disciples of all nations (Matthew 28:19–20; Mark 16:15–18), has been repeated and renewed to the Latter-day Saints: "Go ye into all the world, preach the gospel to every creature, acting in the authority which I have given you, baptizing in the name of the Father, and of the Son, and of the Holy Ghost. (D&C 68:8.)

One president of the Church expressed himself to those not of the LDS faith: "We have come not to take away from you the truth and virtue you possess. We have come not to find fault with you nor criticize you. We have not come here to berate you because of things you have not done; but we have come here as your brethren . . . and to say to you: 'Keep all the good that you have, and let us bring to you more good, in order that you may be happier and in order that you may be prepared to enter into the presence of our Heavenly Father.'"[9]

Those who are content with what they have are perfectly free to express the same to LDS missionaries. Those who are curious, unsatisfied with their present faith or way of life, or those who may be seeking for answers to some of life's puzzling questions, may find an encounter with the Latter-day Saints worth their time and attention.

25. *What do the Latter-day Saints hope to accomplish in the religious world?*

Because the Latter-day Saints are Christian, because they believe that peace and happiness here and hereafter are to be found only in and through the person and powers of Jesus Christ, they also believe that the only hope for the world is to

---

[9] George Albert Smith, *Sharing the Gospel with Others*, compiled by Preston Nibley (Salt Lake City: Deseret Book Co., 1948), pp. 12–13.

come unto Christ. The answer to the world's problems—to the vexing troubles of starvation, famine, disease, crime, inhumanity, and the dissolution of the nuclear family—is ultimately not to be found in more extravagant social programs or stronger legislation. The Latter-day Saints acknowledge and value the good that is done by so many to bring the message of Jesus from the New Testament to a world that desperately needs it. At the same time, they feel to say to a drifting world that there is more truth to be known, more power to be exercised, and more profound fulfillment to be had. As one Church leader pointed out, "We seek to bring all truth together. We seek to enlarge the circle of love and understanding among all the people of the earth. Thus we strive to establish peace and happiness, not only within Christianity but among all mankind."[10]

The capsule summary of the message of The Church of Jesus Christ of Latter-day Saints is that there is a God; Jesus Christ is his divine Son; the Father and the Son have appeared and spoken again in these times; and the Father's plan of salvation has been restored to earth for the ultimate blessing of humankind. In short, the Latter-day Saints believe that God loves his children in this age and generation as much as he loved those to whom he sent his Son in earlier days. God the Father's perfect love is manifest not only through the preservation of the biblical record but also through modern revelation, modern scripture, and modern apostles and prophets.

The Latter-day Saints offer hope to a world strangled with hopelessness. At a time in which there is a waning of belonging, the Latter-day Saints invite all people to come home, to return to the family of God. If some of those who wander or have lost their way can be retrieved and oriented toward their eternal possibilities, then the LDS Church will have had a lasting impact on the world. The First Presidency of the Church in 1907 made the following declaration: "Our

---

[10] Howard W. Hunter, *That We Might Have Joy* (Salt Lake City: Deseret Book Co., 1994), p. 59.

motives are not selfish; our purposes not petty and earth-bound; we contemplate the human race, past, present and yet to come, as immortal beings, for whose salvation it is our mission to labor; and to this work, broad as eternity and deep as the love of God, we devote ourselves, now, and forever."[11]

---

[11] Conference Report, April 1907, appendix, 16; cited in Hunter, *That We Might Have Joy*, p. 59.

THE ARTICLES

OF FAITH

1. We believe in God, the Eternal Father, and in His Son, Jesus Christ, and in the Holy Ghost.

2. We believe that men will be punished for their own sins, and not for Adam's transgression.

3. We believe that through the Atonement of Christ, all mankind may be saved, by obedience to the laws and ordinances of the Gospel.

4. We believe that the first principles and ordinances of the Gospel are: first, Faith in the Lord Jesus Christ; second, Repentance; third, Baptism by immersion for the remission of sins; fourth, Laying on of hands for the gift of the Holy Ghost.

5. We believe that a man must be called of God, by prophecy, and by the laying on of hands by those who are in authority, to preach the Gospel and administer in the ordinances thereof.

6. We believe in the same organization that existed in the Primitive Church, namely, apostles, prophets, pastors, teachers, evangelists, and so forth.

7. We believe in the gift of tongues, prophecy, revelation, visions, healing, interpretation of tongues, and so forth.

8. We believe the Bible to be the word of God as far as it is translated correctly; we also believe the Book of Mormon to be the word of God.

9. We believe all that God has revealed, all that He does now reveal, and we believe that He will yet reveal many great and important things pertaining to the Kingdom of God.

10. We believe in the literal gathering of Israel and in the restoration of the Ten Tribes; that Zion (the New Jerusalem) will be built upon the American continent; that Christ will reign personally upon the earth; and, that the earth will be renewed and receive its paradisiacal glory.

11. We claim the privilege of worshiping Almighty God according to the dictates of our own conscience, and allow all men the same privilege, let them worship how, where, or what they may.

12. We believe in being subject to kings, presidents, rulers, and magistrates, in obeying, honoring, and sustaining the law.

13. We believe in being honest, true, chaste, benevolent, virtuous, and in doing good to all men; indeed, we may say that we follow the admonition of Paul—We believe all things, we hope all things, we have endured many things, and hope to be able to endure all things. If there is anything virtuous, lovely, or of good report or praiseworthy, we seek after these things.

—Joseph Smith [March 1842]

DISTINCTIVE
LDS DOCTRINES

Although the Latter-day Saints love the Bible and are encouraged by their prophet leaders to become serious students of the Bible, they also look for direction to the Book of Mormon, Doctrine and Covenants, Pearl of Great Price, and living prophets. Thus the Latter-day Saints are not dependent upon the Bible alone for doctrine, church organization, or standards of living. In addition, because they are not linked historically to the Christian tradition, either Roman Catholic or Protestant, they are not tied to doctrinal developments, church councils, or creedal statements that grew out of the Christian church's efforts through the centuries to interpret and thereafter explicate its theology. Thus the Latter-day Saints feel no need to "prove" their positions from the Bible or from past or present Christian beliefs or practices.

At the same time, the Latter-day Saints do believe that remnants of some of their more distinctive doctrines and practices can be found in Christian history. In this appendix we will consider very briefly three specific areas: God and his relationship with man; the premortal existence of man; and the practice of baptism for the dead.

1. GOD AND MAN

As mentioned in the body of this work, Latter-day Saints believe that the Godhead consists of three separate and distinct personages—God the Father, his Son Jesus Christ, and the Holy Ghost. On the whole, believing Christians throughout the world accept the proposition that the Holy Ghost is a spirit, and that Jesus did in fact rise from the tomb with a physical, resurrected body. Latter-day Saints believe that God the Father is an exalted man, a Man of Holiness who possesses a physical (corporeal) body. This, of course, is soundly rejected by other Christian denominations. Once again, Latter-day Saints believe this not just because it is taught in the Bible but also because modern prophets have so declared it. The idea that God has a corporeal body was also taught rather extensively in the early Christian church.[1] Adolph Harnack, in his seven-volume work, *The History of Dogma*, has written that during the first two centuries "God was naturally conceived and represented as corporeal," and that it was a rather "popular idea that God had a form and a kind of corporeal existence."[2]

Latter-day Saints reject the doctrine of the Trinity because of the teachings of Joseph Smith concerning the separateness of the three Gods. In addition, the Latter-day Saints feel that the doctrine of the Trinity is unscriptural, that it represents a superimposition of Hellenistic philosophy on the Bible, a creedal concept that came predominantly through the church councils at Nicaea and Chalcedon, and that the simplest and clearest reading of the four Gospels sets forth a Godhead of three distinct beings—not three coequal persons in one substance or essence. Indeed, it is not difficult to find non-LDS biblical scholars who agree that the Trinity is unbiblical. One scholar observed, "There is no formal doctrine of the Trinity

---

[1] See David L. Paulsen, "Early Christian Belief in a Corporeal Deity: Origen and Augustine as Reluctant Witnesses," *Harvard Theological Review* 83:2, 1990, pp. 105–16.

[2] *The History of Dogma*, 7 vols. (New York: Dover, 1961), 1:180, note 1; 2:255, note 5.

in the New Testament writers, if this means an explicit teaching that in one God there are three co-equal divine persons."[3] Latter-day Saints concur that "the word [Trinity] itself does not occur in the Bible. It is generally acknowledged that the church father Tertullian (ca. A.D. 145–220) either coined the term or was the first to use it with reference to God. . . . The formal doctrine of the Trinity as it was defined by the great church councils of the fourth and fifth centuries is not to be found in the New Testament."[4]

The ideas that follow (and biblical references) were prepared by my colleague Thomas Sherry. They represent a fairly typical LDS view of biblical passages regarding the members of the Godhead.[5]

Latter-day Saints believe that taken together, New Testament references to the Godhead bear witness of a Trinity of oneness in purpose, not oneness of essence, and of a Godhead composed of three physically separate beings. The material for this study was developed by cataloging every verse in the King James Version of the New Testament in which more than one member of the Godhead is mentioned. From these references, sixty-five scriptural incidents or doctrinal statements representative of the Godhead relationship were chosen. These references were then categorized according to questions they raised about orthodox creeds of the Trinity. Six major categories were needed to cover the questions. Each scripture was also compared to the seven other English translations of the Bible found in Tyndale's Eight-Translation New Testament (New English Bible, Jerusalem Bible, Living Bible, Today's English Version, New International Version, Philips Modern English, and Revised Standard Version). Interest-

---

[3] Edward J. Fortman, *The Triune God: A Historical Study of the Doctrine of the Trinity* (Philadelphia: Westminster Press, 1972), p. 32.

[4] *Harper's Bible Dictionary*, edited by Paul J. Achtemeier (San Francisco: Harper & Row, 1985), pp. 1,098–99.

[5] Adapted from "Scripturally Questioning the Traditional Sectarian View of the Trinity," in *The Eighth Annual Church Educational System Religious Educators' Symposium* (Salt Lake City: The Church of Jesus Christ of Latter-day Saints, 1984), pp. 147–49.

ingly, only two of the sixty-five scriptures (Matthew 19:16–17 and Philippines 2:5–9) were translated so differently as to render them invalid as examples of the category under which they were placed. In both cases the Living Bible rendition was the translation that invalidated their use.

In the first category were placed scriptures that express the will of the Son as being different from or in subjection to the will of the Father: Matthew 26:39; Mark 14:36; Luke 22:42; and John 4:34; 5:30; 6:38–40. The question raised by these scriptures is, If Jesus Christ and God the Father are the same beings in whom continually dwells the fullness of perfection, how could the will of the Son be at variance with or in subjection to the will of the Father?

In a second category are placed scriptures that suggest that the Father has power, knowledge, glory, and dominion (including the right and powers to direct that dominion) that the Son does not have and to which the Son is in subjection. The scriptures and the questions they raise are numerous. They include Mark 13:32 (cf. Matthew 24:36); Luke 18:18–19 (cf. Matthew 19:16–17; 23:7–9; Mark 10:17–18); Luke 22:29; 23:34; John 5:19–27, 37 (cf. John 8:26–29; 12:49–50); John 8:42; 10:17–18; 11:41–42; 14:28; 15:9–10, 15; Acts 10:38, 40; 1 Corinthians 11:3; 15:28; Philippians 2:5–9; Hebrews 1:1–4 (cf. Matthew 21:38; John 3:35; Romans 8:17 [How can Christ be an heir to that which he already possesses? What does the word inheritance mean if Jesus already owns, or possesses, everything?]); Hebrews 1:5 (cf. 2 Corinthians 11:31; 1 Peter 1:3 [These scriptures talk about Jesus' having a Father who is also his God. How can this be if there is only one God and the Trinity is one being?]); and Hebrews 5:1–10 (How can these differences exist if the Father and the Son are the same being? Even if that same being is performing in different roles, how can he have more or less actual power or knowledge in one role than in another? Why did Jesus need counsel from the Father if they are the same being?).

The entire seventeenth chapter of the Gospel of John—Christ's great intercessory prayer—loses its impact and meaning if the Father is the same being as the Son. Why plead for unity if the kind of unity expressed in verse 11 is, according to the creeds, not possible? Can all believers become the same being as Jesus and God ("that they may be one, as we are" [John 17:11])? It seems most plausible that the unity spoken of here is one of witness and purpose rather than of essence.

The third category contains scriptures that indicate that Jesus needed help and a sustaining power from the Father to perform his mission on earth. The scriptures in this category are Matthew 26:37–44 (cf. Mark 14:33–39; Luke 22:41–45); Matthew 14:23; 27:46 (cf. Mark 15:34); and Luke 6:12. Some questions raised by these verses are, If God the Father and Jesus are the same being, why would the Son need help from himself? Why would he pray to himself?

The fourth category contains scriptures that suggest that the Father, the Son, and the Holy Ghost were simultaneously in different locations: Matthew 3:13–17 (cf. Mark 1:10–11; Luke 3:21–22); Matthew 17:5 (cf. Mark 9:7; Luke 9:28–36); John 12:28–30; 15:26; 20:17; Acts 7:55–56. The question here is not whether God could conceivably be simultaneously in different locations, but rather, why would he want to give a confusing and apparently deceptive impression?

The fifth category is composed of scriptures expressing the mediation of Christ. These are Matthew 11:25–27 (cf. Luke 10:21–22); John 14:6; 1 Timothy 2:5; Hebrews 7:25; and 1 John 2:1. The question raised by these scriptures is, Why is there a need for Christ to act as a mediator between man and the Father if Christ is the Father?

The sixth category is made up of miscellaneous scriptures that indicate the distinct natures of the Father and the Son:

Matthew 16:15–17. If Jesus, who at this time was "flesh and blood," did not reveal his own Messiahship to Peter, who did?

Luke 2:52. How could Jesus grow in favor with himself? How could he gain wisdom if he possessed all wisdom before?

Luke 23:46. Why would Christ commend his spirit to himself?

John 7:16–17. How could his doctrine not be his if he is the same being as the Father?

John 16:27–30 (see all of chapter 16). When viewed in light of John 8:42, this scripture also answers the apostles' query about the relationship of Jesus to God the Father. What sense would this scripture make if one substituted the word Jesus for each use of the words, I, me, and Father? Why does Paul consistently open each of his letters with a statement emphasizing the separateness of God the Father and his Son, Jesus Christ—particularly since all of these letters were written after the Resurrection? (See Romans 1:1–3; 1 Corinthians 1:3; 2 Corinthians 1:2–3; Galatians 1:1–4; Ephesians 1:2–3; Philippians 1:1–2; Colossians 1:2–3; 1 Thessalonians 1:1; 2 Thessalonians 1:1–2; 1 Timothy 1:2; 2 Timothy 1:2; Titus 1:4; Philemon 1:3; and Hebrews 1:1–2, 5.)

That the Holy Ghost is a being physically separate from the Father and Son is evidenced in these references: Matthew 12:31–32 (here it seems that a certain type of sin against Christ is forgivable, but against the Holy Ghost it is not); John 14:26 (cf. Luke 11:13; John 16:7); and Acts 10:38 (if they are the same being, how can God anoint himself with himself?).

In short, Latter-day Saints believe that the simplest reading of the New Testament text produces the simplest conclusion—that the Father, the Son, and the Holy Ghost are separate and distinct personages, that they are one in purpose, one in mind, one in glory, but separate in person. The sheer preponderance of references in the Bible would lead an uninformed reader—one unaffected by either the conclusions of the creeds (Protestant and Catholic positions) or insights from latter-day revelation (LDS position)—to the understanding that God the Father, Jesus Christ, and the Holy Ghost are separate beings. That is, one must look to the third- and fourth-century Christian church, not to the New Testament itself, to make a strong case for the Trinity.

Finally, Joseph Smith taught (and Latter-day Saints believe) that men and women have the capacity to eventually become as God is. This doctrine is particularly distasteful to some Christians who feel it in some way robs Deity of his omnipotence. To be sure, we will forevermore worship and adore God the Father and Jesus Christ the Savior, no matter how much we may grow and develop spiritually in time or in eternity. They nevertheless believe that the plan of salvation was put into operation to achieve that very end—to enable God's spirit children to become as he is.

The doctrine of the deification of man—that human beings can, through the atoning sacrifice of Jesus Christ and through the divine transformation of human nature, become joint heirs or co-inheritors with Christ to all the Father has— was clearly taught in the early Christian church.[6] One major reference work explains, "Deification (Greek *theosis*) is for Orthodoxy the goal of every Christian. Man, according to the Bible, is 'made in the image and likeness of God.' . . . It is possible for man to become like God, to become deified, to become god by grace. . . . It should be noted that deification does not mean absorption into God, since the deified creature remains itself and distinct. It is the whole human being, body and soul, who is transfigured in the Spirit into the likeness of the divine nature, and deification is the goal of every Christian."[7]

Note the following from early Christian thinkers:

Irenaeus, bishop of Lyons (ca. A.D. 130–200): "Do we cast blame on [God] because we were not made gods from the beginning, but were at first created merely as men, and then later as gods?" Also: "But man receives progression and increase towards God. For as God is always the same, so also man, when found in God, shall always progress toward God."[8]

Clement of Alexandria (ca. A.D. 150–215): "If one knows himself, he will know God and knowing God will become like God."[9]

---

[6] I am indebted to the work of my colleague Stephen E. Robinson in *Are Mormons Christian?* (Salt Lake City: Bookcraft, 1991), pp. 60–65, for much of what follows.
[7] Symeon Lash, "Deification," in *The Westminster Dictionary of Christian Theology,* edited by Alan Richardson and John Bowden (Philadelphia: Westminster Press, 1983), pp. 147–48.
[8] *Against Heresies* 4.38; 4.11.
[9] *The Instructor* 3.1; see also *Stromateis,* 23.

Athanasius, bishop of Alexandria (ca. A.D. 296–373): "The word was made flesh in order that we might be enabled to be made gods. . . . Just as the Lord, putting on the body, became a man, so also we men are both deified through his flesh, and henceforth inherit everlasting life."[10]

Augustine of Hippo (ca. A.D. 354–430): "He himself that justifies also deifies, for by justifying he makes sons of God. 'For he has given them power to become the sons of God' (John 1:12). If then we have been made sons of God, we have also been made gods."[11]

All men and women, like Christ, are made in the image and likeness of God (Genesis 1:27; Pearl of Great Price, Moses 2:27), and so it is neither robbery nor heresy for the children of God to aspire to be like God (Matthew 5:48; Philippians 2:6); like any parent, our Heavenly Father would want his children to become and be all that he is. Godhood comes through overcoming the world through the Atonement of Christ (1 John 5:4–5; Revelation 2:7, 11; D&C 76:51–60), becoming heirs of God and joint-heirs with the Savior, who is the natural Heir (Romans 8:17; Galatians 4:7), and thus inheriting *all* things, just as Christ inherits all things (1 Corinthians 3:21–23; Revelation 21:7; D&C 76:55, 95; 84:38; 88:107). The faithful are received into the "church of the Firstborn" (Hebrews 12:23; D&C 76:54, 67, 94; 93:22), meaning they inherit as though they were the firstborn. In that glorified state we will be conformed to the image of the Lord (Romans 8:29; 1 Corinthians 15:49; 2 Corinthians 3:18; 1 John 3:2; Book of Mormon, Alma 5:14), receive his glory, and be one with him and with the Father (John 17:21–23; Philippians 3:21).

2. THE PREMORTAL EXISTENCE OF MAN

As indicated in chapter 5, Latter-day Saints believe that God revealed to Joseph Smith, as a part of the restoration of

---

[10] *Against the Arians* 1.39; 3:34.
[11] *On the Psalms* 50.2.

all things, the knowledge that men and women have always lived—more specifically, that we lived before we were born on this earth in a mortal condition.[12] They teach that this life is but Act Two of a three-act play, and that life here makes sense only as viewed in that overall theological context.

The doctrine of the preexistence of man appears to have been taught in the Christian Church until at least the sixth century A.D. Some of these early Christian thinkers suggested, as do the Latter-day Saints today, that mortality can be understood only in terms of labors and assignments and agreements in the premortal world. Papias, bishop of Hierapolis in Asia Minor (ca. A.D. 130–140), in speaking of the leaders of the early Christian church, wrote, "To some of them, that is, those angels [spirits] who had been faithful to God in former times, [God] gave supervision over the governments of the earth, trusting or commissioning them to rule well. . . . And nothing has occurred [since] to put an end to their order."[13] In referring to Jeremiah 1:5 in regard to Jeremiah's being known by God before Jeremiah was born, Clement of Alexandria wrote, "It is possible that in speaking these things the prophet is referring to us, as being known to God as faithful before the foundation of the world."[14]

Origen of Alexandria (ca. A.D. 185–254) discoursed at length about the premortal existence of souls. He spoke of the soul "as being 'akin' to God, but obliged to live in a material world which is not its true home." Further, "The material world is for Origen temporary and provisional, and life in it is a short period in a much longer life of the soul, which exists before being united to the body and will continue hereafter."[15] Origen postulated that "the individual soul preexists its

---

[12] I am indebted to my friend and colleague Brent L. Top for his book *The Life Before* (Salt Lake City: Bookcraft, 1988), an important work that sets forth at some length an LDS perspective on this doctrine. I have relied heavily upon the material in chapter 2.

[13] *Patrologogiae Cursus Completus . . . Series Graeca* 5:1260.

[14] *Patrologiae . . . Graeca* 8:321.

[15] Henry Chadwick, *The Early Church*, rev. ed. (New York: Penguin, 1993), pp. 101, 105.

embodiment as a human being." Thus "it is the soul, 'the inner person,' and not . . . the body, that is the seat of that which corresponds to the image of God." Origen thus regarded the soul "as the real human person."[16]

"It was [Origen's] belief that the many differences seen among men on earth could be traced back to the differences in rank and glory of the premortal angels. Without such a belief in a premortal existence, he maintained, it would not be possible to view God as 'no respecter of persons,' but rather God would seem arbitrary, cruel, and unjust. Origen believed that the differences between men on earth, as with the 'angels,' were based on merit. Just as there would be a judgment at the end of man's earth life, Origen believed that some sort of judgment had already taken place before we came here which was based on work done in a premortal state. In applying this principle to Jacob's being preferred over Esau, Origen wrote, 'We believe that he was even then chosen by God because of merits acquired before this life.'"[17] Origen's teachings were eventually rejected by the Roman emperor Justinian in A.D. 543 as speculative and too interwoven with Greek thought. "Yet Christianity's debt to Origen is immense," W. H. C. Frend has written. "No Christian writer had attempted so thorough and complete a statement of this [Christian] religion. No one before him had defended it so thoroughly against its opponents, and with such success."[18]

Again, the LDS belief in preexistence is founded on modern revelation, what Joseph Smith and his successors have taught. But it is clear that this doctrine is found not only in Christian history but also in such varied sources as the teachings of the Essene community,[19] the pseudepigraphic Book of Enoch,[20]

---

[16] *Encyclopedia of Early Christianity,* edited by Everett Ferguson (New York: Garland Publishing Co., 1990), p. 863.

[17] Top, *The Life Before,* p. 18.

[18] *The Rise of Christianity* (Philadelphia: Fortress Press, 1984), p. 382.

[19] Josephus, *Antiquities of the Jews* 15:371; *The Jewish Wars* 2:154–56.

[20] See comments from R. H. Charles in *The Apocrypha and Pseudepigrapha of the Old Testament* 2:444.

the First Apocalypse of James,[21] and the Syriac Hymn of the Pearl.[22]

Biblical passages that refer to the premortal existence include:

1. The premortal existence of Jesus Christ. (John 1:1–2, 14; 6:38, 51, 62; 8:56–59; 16:28–30; 17:4–5; Hebrews 1:1–3; 1 Peter 1:18–20.)

2. The premortal existence of men and women. (Numbers 16:22; 27:16; Deuteronomy 32:7–9; Job 38:4–7; Ecclesiastes 12:7; Jeremiah 1:4–5; Zechariah 12:1; Acts 17:26–27.)

3. The fall of Lucifer in the premortal world. (Isaiah 14:12–15; Luke 10:17–18; 2 Peter 2:4; Jude 1:6; Revelation 12:7–12.)

3. BAPTISM FOR THE DEAD

Latter-day Saints believe that baptism for the dead was indeed a practice of the Church of Jesus Christ in the meridian of time, a practice that was restored in the last days through Joseph Smith. The Apostle Paul refers to baptism for the dead in 1 Corinthians. Chapter 15, perhaps the most potent chapter doctrinally in the epistle, testifies of the resurrection of the Lord. In it Paul presented the core of that message known to us as the gospel, or the "glad tidings" that Christ atoned for our sins, died, rose again the third day, and ascended into heaven. Joseph Smith called these events "the fundamental principles of our religion," to which all other doctrines are but appendages.[23] Paul showed the necessity for the Savior's rising from the tomb and explained that the physical evidence of the divine Sonship of Christ is the resurrection. If Christ had not risen from the dead, Paul asserted, the preaching of the apostles and the faith of the Saints would be in vain. "If in this life only we have hope in Christ," he said, "we are of all men most miserable." (1 Corinthians 15:19.)

---

[21] See William Schneemelcher, ed., *New Testament Apocrypha*, 2 vols., rev. ed. (Louisville, Kentucky: Westminster/John Knox Press, 1991), 1:323.

[22] See ibid., 3:380–85.

[23] *Teachings*, p. 121.

After establishing that the Lord has conquered all enemies, including death, Paul added, "And when all things shall
be subdued unto him, then shall the Son also himself be subject unto him [the Father] that put all things under him, that
God may be all in all. *Else what shall they do which are baptized
for the dead, if the dead rise not at all? why are they then baptized for
the dead?*" (1 Corinthians 15:28–29; emphasis added.) Verse
29 has spawned a host of interpretations by biblical scholars
of various faiths. Many consider the original meaning of the
passage to be at best "difficult" or "unclear." One commenta-
tor stated that Paul "alludes to a practice of the Corinthian
community as evidence for Christian faith in the resurrection
of the dead. It seems that in Corinth some Christians would
undergo baptism in the name of their deceased non-Christian
relatives and friends, hoping that this vicarious baptism might
assure them a share in the redemption of Christ."[24] Some
recent translations of the Bible have attempted to clarify this
passage. The New King James Version has it: "Otherwise,
what will they do who are baptized for the dead, if the dead
do not rise at all? Why then are they baptized for the dead?"
The Revised English Bible translates 1 Corinthians 15:29 in
this way: "Again, there are those who receive baptism on
behalf of the dead. What do you suppose they are doing? If
the dead are not raised to life at all, what do they mean by
being baptized on their behalf?"

Some non–Latter-day Saints believe that in 1 Corinthians
Paul was denouncing or condemning the practice of baptism
for the dead as heretical. This is a strange conclusion, since
Paul used the practice of baptism for the dead to support the
doctrine of the resurrection. In essence, he says, "Why are we
performing baptism in behalf of our dead, if, as some propose,
there will be no resurrection of the dead? If there is to be no
resurrection, would not such baptisms be a waste of time?"
On the subject of baptism for the dead, one Latter-day Saint

---

[24] Richard Kugelman, "The First Letter to the Corinthians," in *The Jerome Biblical
Commentary*, 2 vols., ed. Raymond E. Brown, Joseph A. Fitzmyer, and Roland E.
Murphy (Englewood Cliffs, N.J.: Prentice-Hall, 1968), 2:273.

writer observed, "Paul was most sensitive to blasphemy and false ceremonialism—of all people he would not have argued for the foundation truth of the resurrection with a questionable example. He obviously did not feel that the principle was disharmonious with the gospel."[25]

A surprising amount of evidence suggests that the doctrine of salvation for the dead was known and understood by ancient Christian communities. Early commentary on the statement in Hebrews that "they without us should not be made perfect" (Hebrews 11:40) holds that the passage referred to the Old Testament Saints who were trapped in Hades awaiting the help of their New Testament counterparts, and that Christ held the keys that would "open the doors of the Underworld to the faithful souls there."[26] It is significant that in his work *Dialogue with Trypho,* Justin Martyr, the early Christian apologist (ca. A.D. 100–165), cites an apocryphon that he charges had been deleted from the book of Jeremiah but was still to be found in some synagogue copies of the text: "The Lord God remembered His dead people of Israel who lay in the graves; and He descended to preach to them His own salvation."[27] Irenaeus also taught, "The Lord descended to the parts under the earth, announcing to them also the good news of his coming, there being remission of sins for such as believe on him."[28]

One of the early Christian documents linking the writings of Peter on Christ's ministry in the spirit world (see 1 Peter 3:18–20; 4:6) with those of Paul on baptism for the dead is the "Shepherd of Hermas," which states that "these apostles and teachers who preached the name of the Son of God, having fallen asleep in the power and faith of the Son of God,

---

[25] Richard Lloyd Anderson, *Understanding Paul* (Salt Lake City: Deseret Book Co., 1983), p. 405.

[26] J. A. MacCulloch, *The Harrowing of Hell* (Edinburgh, Scotland: T. & T. Clark, 1930), pp. 48–49.

[27] Ibid., pp. 84–85; also in *The Ante-Nicene Fathers,* 10 vols. (Grand Rapids, Mich.: Wm. B. Eerdmans Publishing Co., 1951), 1:235.

[28] Irenaeus, *Against Heresies* 4.27.1, in J. B. Lightfoot, *The Apostolic Fathers* (Grand Rapids, Mich.: Baker Book House, 1962), pp. 277–78.

preached also to those who had fallen asleep before them, and themselves gave to them the seal of the preaching. *They went down therefore with them into the water and came up again,* but the latter went down alive and came up alive, while the former, who had fallen asleep before, went down dead but came up alive. *Through them, therefore, they were made alive, and received the knowledge of the name of the Son of God."*[29]

It is of much interest to me that this question of the range and depth and extent of Christ's saving gospel—including the possibility of the gospel being taught to and received by those who have died—has begun to receive a surprising amount of attention by modern Christian thinkers as well. One writer asks, "What is the fate of those who die never hearing the gospel of Christ? Are all the 'heathen' lost? Is there an opportunity for those who have never heard of Jesus to be saved?

"These questions raise one of the most perplexing, provocative and perennial issues facing Christians. It has been considered by philosophers and farmers, Christians and non-Christians. In societies where Christianity has had strong influence, just about everyone has either asked or been asked about the final destiny of those dying without knowledge of the only Savior, Jesus Christ. Far and away, this is the most-asked apologetic question on U.S. college campuses." The author then proceeds, with other contributors, to discuss this rather difficult issue.[30]

---

[29] *The Shepherd of Hermas,* similitude 9.16.2–4 (Loeb Classical Library, translated by Kirsopp Lake); cited in Anderson, *Understanding Paul,* pp. 407–8; emphasis added

[30] John Sanders, ed., *What About Those Who Never Heard? Three Views on the Destiny of the Unevangelized* (Downers Grove, Ill.: InterVarsity Press, 1995), p. 7; see also John Sanders, *No Other Name: An Investigation into the Destiny of the Unevangelized* (Grand Rapids, Mich.: Eerdmans Publishing Co., 1992); Dennis L. Okholm and Timothy R. Phillips, eds., *Four Views on Salvation in a Pluralistic World* (Grand Rapids, Mich.: Zondervan Publishing House, 1995); see also a critique of the position that suggests the possibility of salvation beyond the grave in Millard J. Erickson, *How Shall They Be Saved? The Destiny of Those Who Do Not Hear of Jesus* (Grand Rapids, Mich.: Baker Books, 1996). Oddly enough, the LDS position on the redemption of the dead is not mentioned by any of the authors.

PRESIDENTS OF THE CHURCH OF JESUS CHRIST OF LATTER-DAY SAINTS

Joseph Smith, Jr.	1830–1844
Brigham Young	1847–1877
John Taylor	1880–1887
Wilford Woodruff	1889–1898
Lorenzo Snow	1898–1901
Joseph F. Smith	1901–1918
Heber J. Grant	1918–1945
George Albert Smith	1945–1951
David O. McKay	1951–1970
Joseph Fielding Smith	1970–1972
Harold B. Lee	1972–1973
Spencer W. Kimball	1973–1985
Ezra Taft Benson	1985–1994
Howard W. Hunter	1994–1995
Gordon B. Hinckley	1995–

Statement of the First Presidency (1978)

February 1978

Based upon ancient and modern revelation, The Church of Jesus Christ of Latter-day Saints gladly teaches and declares the Christian doctrine that all men and women are brothers and sisters, not only by blood relationship from common mortal progenitors, but also as literal spirit children of an Eternal Father.

The great religious leaders of the world such as Mohammed, Confucius, and the Reformers, as well as philosophers including Socrates, Plato, and others, received a portion of God's light. Moral truths were given to them by God to enlighten whole nations and to bring a higher level of understanding to individuals.

The Hebrew prophets prepared the way for the coming of Jesus Christ, the promised Messiah, who should provide salvation for all mankind who believe in the gospel.

Consistent with these truths, we believe that God has given and will give to all peoples sufficient knowledge to help them on their way to eternal salvation, either in this life or in the life to come.

We also declare that the gospel of Jesus Christ, restored to his Church in our day, provides the only way to a mortal life of happiness and a fullness of joy forever. For those who have not received the gospel, the opportunity will come to them in the life hereafter if not in this life.

Our message therefore is one of special love and concern for the eternal welfare of all men and women, regardless of religious belief, race, or nationality, knowing that we are truly brothers and sisters because we are the sons and daughters of the same Eternal Father.

Spencer W. Kimball
N. Eldon Tanner
Marion G. Romney
THE FIRST PRESIDENCY

APPENDIX 5

PROCLAMATION OF THE FIRST PRESIDENCY AND THE QUORUM OF THE TWELVE APOSTLES (1980)

The Church of Jesus Christ of Latter-day Saints was organized 150 years ago today. On this sesquicentennial anni-
versary we issue to the world a proclamation concerning its
progress, its doctrine, its mission, and its message.

On April 6, 1830, a small group assembled in the farm-
house of Peter Whitmer in Fayette Township in the State of
New York. Six men participated in the formal organization
procedures, with Joseph Smith as their leader. From that
modest beginning in a rural area, this work has grown consistently and broadly, as men and women in many lands have
embraced the doctrine and entered the waters of baptism. . . .

We testify that this restored gospel was introduced into
the world by the marvelous appearance of God the Eternal
Father and His Son, the resurrected Lord Jesus Christ. That
most glorious manifestation marked the beginning of the

fulfillment of the promise of Peter, who prophesied of "the times of restitution of all things, which God hath spoken by the mouth of all his holy prophets since the world began," this in preparation for the coming of the Lord to reign personally upon the earth (Acts 3:21).

We solemnly affirm that The Church of Jesus Christ of Latter-day Saints is in fact a restoration of the Church established by the Son of God, when in mortality he organized his work upon the earth; that it carries his sacred name, even the name of Jesus Christ; that it is built upon a foundation of Apostles and prophets, he being the chief cornerstone; that its priesthood, in both the Aaronic and Melchizedek orders, was restored under the hands of those who held it anciently: John the Baptist, in the case of the Aaronic; and Peter, James, and John in the case of the Melchizedek.

We declare that the Book of Mormon was brought forth by the gift and power of God and that it stands beside the Bible as another witness of Jesus the Christ, the Savior and Redeemer of mankind. Together they testify of his divine Sonship.

We give our witness that the doctrines and practices of the Church encompass salvation and exaltation not only for those who are living, but also for the dead, and that in sacred temples built for this purpose a great vicarious work is going forward in behalf of those who have died, so that all men and women of all generations may become the beneficiaries of the saving ordinances of the gospel of the Master. This great, selfless labor is one of the distinguishing features of this restored Church of Jesus Christ.

We affirm the sanctity of the family as a divine creation and declare that God our Eternal Father will hold parents accountable to rear their children in light and truth, teaching them "to pray, and to walk uprightly before the Lord" (D&C 68:28). We teach that the most sacred of all relationships, those family associations of husbands and wives and parents and children, may be continued eternally when marriage is solemnized under the authority of the holy priesthood exercised in temples dedicated for these divinely authorized purposes.

We bear witness that all men and women are sons and daughters of God, each accountable to him; that our lives here on earth are part of an eternal plan; that death is not the end, but rather a transition from this to another sphere of purposeful activity made possible through the Atonement of the Redeemer of the world; and that we shall there have the opportunity of working and growing toward perfection.

We testify that the spirit of prophecy and revelation is among us. "We believe all that God has revealed, all that He does now reveal; and we believe that He will yet reveal many great and important things pertaining to the Kingdom of God" (Pearl of Great Price, Articles of Faith 1:9). The heavens are not sealed; God continues to speak to his children through a prophet empowered to declare his word, now as he did anciently.

The mission of the Church today, as it has been from the beginning, is to teach the gospel of Christ to all the world in obedience to the commandment given by the Savior prior to his ascension and repeated in modern revelation: "Go ye into all the world, preach the gospel to every creature, acting in the authority which I have given you, baptizing in the name of the Father, and of the Son, and of the Holy Ghost" (D&C 68:8).

Through the Prophet Joseph Smith the Lord revealed these words of solemn warning:

> Hearken ye people from afar; and ye that are upon the islands of the sea, listen together. For verily, the voice of the Lord is unto all men, and there is none to escape; and there is no eye that shall not see, neither ear that shall not hear, neither heart that shall not be penetrated. And the rebellious shall be pierced with much sorrow; for their iniquities shall be spoken upon the housetops, and their secret acts shall be revealed. And the voice of warning shall be unto all people, by the mouths of my disciples, whom I have chosen in these last days. [D&C 1:1–4.]

It is our obligation, therefore, to teach faith in the Lord Jesus Christ, to plead with the people of the earth for individual repentance, to administer the sacred ordinances of baptism by immersion for the remission of sins and the laying on of hands for the gift of the Holy Ghost—all of this under the authority of the priesthood of God.

It is our responsibility to espouse and follow an inspired program of instruction and activity, and to build and maintain appropriate facilities for the accomplishment of this, that all who will hear and accept may grow in understanding of doctrine and develop in principles of Christian service to their fellowmen.

As we stand today on the summit of 150 years of progress, we contemplate humbly and gratefully the sacrifices of those who have gone before us, many of whom gave their lives in testimony of this truth. We are thankful for their faith, for their example, for their mighty labors and willing consecrations for this cause which they considered more precious than life itself. They have passed to us a remarkable heritage. We are resolved to build on that heritage for the blessing and benefit of those who follow, who will constitute ever enlarging numbers of faithful men and women throughout the earth.

This is God's work. It is his kingdom we are building. Anciently the prophet Daniel spoke of it as a stone cut out of the mountain without hands, which was to roll forth to fill the whole earth (see Daniel 2:31–45). We invite the honest in heart everywhere to listen to the teachings of our missionaries who are sent forth as messengers of eternal truth, to study and learn, and to ask God, our Eternal Father, in the name of his Son, the Lord Jesus Christ, if these things are true.

> And if ye shall ask with a sincere heart, with real intent, having faith in Christ, he will manifest the truth of it unto you, by the power of the Holy Ghost. And by the power of the Holy Ghost ye may know the truth of all things. [Moroni 10:4–5.]

We call upon all men and women to forsake evil and turn to God; to work together to build that brotherhood which must be recognized when we truly come to know that God is our Father and we are his children; and to worship him and his Son, the Lord Jesus Christ, the Savior of mankind. In the authority of the Holy Priesthood in us vested, we bless the seekers of truth wherever they may be and invoke the favor of the Almighty upon all men and nations whose God is the Lord, in the name of Jesus Christ, amen.

PROCLAMATION ON THE FAMILY (1995)

September 1995

First Presidency/Council of the Twelve Apostles

We, the First Presidency and the Council of the Twelve Apostles of The Church of Jesus Christ of Latter-day Saints, solemnly proclaim that marriage between a man and a woman is ordained of God and that the family is central to the Creator's plan for the eternal destiny of His children.

All human beings—male and female—are created in the image of God. Each is a beloved spirit son or daughter of heavenly parents, and, as such, each has a divine nature and destiny. Gender is an essential characteristic of individual premortal, mortal, and eternal identity and purpose.

In the premortal realm, spirit sons and daughters knew and worshipped God as their Eternal Father and accepted His plan by which His children could obtain a physical body and gain earthly experience to progress toward perfection and ultimately realize his or her divine destiny as an heir of eternal life. The divine plan of happiness enables family relationships to be perpetuated beyond the grave. Sacred ordinances and covenants available in holy temples make it possible for individuals to return to the presence of God and for families to be united eternally.

The first commandment that God gave to Adam and Eve pertained to their potential for parenthood as husband and wife. We declare that God's commandment for His children to multiply and replenish the earth remains in force. We further declare that God has commanded that the sacred powers of procreation are to be employed only between man and woman, lawfully wedded as husband and wife.

We declare the means by which mortal life is created to be divinely appointed. We affirm the sanctity of life and of its importance in God's eternal plan.

Husband and wife have a solemn responsibility to love and care for each other and for their children. "Children are an heritage of the Lord." (Psalms 127:3.) Parents have a sacred duty to rear their children in love and righteousness, to provide for their physical and spiritual needs, to teach them to love and serve one another, to observe the commandments of God and to be law-abiding citizens wherever they live. Husbands and wives—mothers and fathers—will be held accountable before God for the discharge of these obligations.

The family is ordained of God. Marriage between man and woman is essential to His eternal plan. Children are entitled to birth within the bonds of matrimony, and to be reared by a father and a mother who honor marital vows with complete fidelity. Happiness in family life is most likely to be achieved when founded upon the teachings of the Lord Jesus Christ. Successful marriages and families are established and maintained on principles of faith, prayer, repentance, forgiveness, respect, love, compassion, work and wholesome recreational activities. By divine design, fathers are to preside over their families in love and righteousness and are responsible to provide the necessities of life and protection for their families. Mothers are primarily responsible for the nurture of their children. In these sacred responsibilities, fathers and mothers are obligated to help one another as equal partners. Disability, death or other circumstances may necessitate individual adaptation. Extended families should lend support when needed.

We warn that individuals who violate covenants of chastity, who abuse spouse or offspring, or who fail to fulfill family responsibilities will one day stand accountable before God. Further, we warn that the disintegration of the family will bring upon individuals, communities and nations the calamities foretold by ancient and modern prophets.

We call upon responsible citizens and officers of government everywhere to promote those measures designed to maintain and strengthen the family as the fundamental unit of society.

INDEX

Blacks and priesthood, 177–78
Blessings, priesthood, 92–93
Body, physical: of God the
    Father, 7–8, 29–30, 58, 169–70;
    as blessing, 36, 59–60
Book of Commandments, 23
Book of Mormon, 20–23, 114,
    170–71, 206
Born again, 83–84, 171–72
Branch, 109
Brigham Young University, 96,
    180
Brownson, Orestes, 2
Bushman, Richard, 22

Calvary, 49–50. *See also* Golgotha
Calvin, John, 165
Campbell, Alexander, 2–3
Campbell, Thomas, 2–3
Cancer, 148
Canon of scripture: doctoral
    course discusses, 13–14; LDS,
    19, 24; adding to, 165–66
Carthage, Illinois, 11
Celestial kingdom, 66–67, 84, 89,
    161–62, 176
Chapels, 87
Children: not accountable for sin,
    33; sealed to parents, 89;
    blessing of, 92
Christianity: before Christ, 43–
    48; Jewish roots of, 113;
    should focus on Christ, 140;
    LDS place in, 164, 181
Christianity Today, 151
Church Education System, 95
Church of Jesus Christ of Latter-
    day Saints, The: basic beliefs
    of, 1, 182, 185–86; organiza-
    tion of, 10, 94, 205; growth of,
    10–12, 148–50; mission of, 95–
    98, 181–83; lay clergy of, 98–
    100; presiding authorities of,

100–102, 201; role of, 102–3,
    166–67; constancy and change
    in, 127, 172–73; reasons for
    growth of, 149–52; not all will
    join, during Millennium, 159;
    neither Catholic nor Protes-
    tant, 163–64; as only true
    church, 165; and RLDS
    church, 167; financial strength
    of, 179–80
Clement of Alexandria, 175
Communion, 85–86
Confirmation, 83–84
Consecration, 105–6
Cornelius, 83
Council on the Disposition of
    Tithes, 102
Covenant: defined, 69–70, 168;
    with Christ, 71–74; baptis-
    mal, 82–83; sacramental, 85;
    endowment, 87–88; with
    house of Israel, 114, 125
Cowdery, Oliver, 25, 124, 130
Cross, 49–50, 168
Cult, 173

Davies, Paul, 145
Davies, W. D., 113, 114
Dead, temple work for, 89–92,
    97–98
Death, 63–64; results from the
    Fall, 33, 48–49; relationship
    with loved ones after, 41–42;
    Christ overcame, 49–52; as
    new phase in life, 62; reunion
    with loved ones after, 150;
    during Millennium, 156–57,
    159
Dispensation, 44–45, 165
Divorce, 144–45
Doctrine and Covenants, 23–24,
    26

Holy Ghost: as member of Godhead, 28–29, 192; characteris-
tics of, 31–32; receiving gift of,
83–84, 171–72
Home teaching, 96–97
House of Israel. *See* Israel

Immersion, baptism by, 81–82
Immortality, 52
Independence, Missouri, 11, 107,
110, 167
"Invictus," answer to, 78–79
Irenaeus, 175
Isaac, 114, 174
Israel: LDS ties with ancient,
113–14; chosen lineage of,
114–18; scattering of, 119–20;
gathering of, 120–23

Jacob, 114, 116, 123, 172
Jehovah, 30, 171. *See also* Jesus
Christ
Jesus Christ: appears to Joseph
Smith, 7–8; visits American
continent, 21–22; as member
of Godhead, 28–29, 188; char-
acteristics of, 30–31, 160; resurrection of, 40, 51, 66; role of,
known to ancient prophets,
43–48; divinity of, 45, 139–40;
atonement of, 49–50, 168; salvation through, 52–54, 75–78,
168–69; in premortal life, 57–
58; changes people, 70; justifies people, 71–74; as captain
of the soul, 78–79; baptism
symbolic of, 81; introduces
sacrament, 85; preaches gospel
in spirit world, 90–91; second
coming of, 154–57; all will
acknowledge, during Millennium, 159, 161; LDS belief in,
164, 167, 181–82; as central

figure in Book of Mormon,
171; on sacred matters, 174;
becoming joint heirs with, 176
John the Baptist, priesthood
restored through, 10, 98
Joseph Smith Translation of
Bible, 25–26, 105
Judgment, 66–68, 162
Justification, 70–74

Kimball, Heber C., 32
Kimball, Spencer W.: declaration
by, included in D&C, 24; on
absolute truth, 37; on suffering, 62–63; on gathering, 110–
11; on Zion, 112; receives revelation allowing blacks to
hold priesthood, 177
Kingdoms of glory, 66–67, 162
Kirtland, Ohio, 11, 124

Lamanites, 21–22, 106–7
Lang, Bernhard, 150
Latter-day Saints. *See* Church of
Jesus Christ of Latter-day
Saints, The
Lay clergy, 98–100
Laying on of hands, 83–84
Lee, Harold B.: on lineage of
Israel, 116–17; on foreordina-
tion, 119; on learning by faith,
132; organizes welfare pro-
gram, 146
Lee, Rex E., 99–100
Levitical Priesthood, 177
Lewis, C. S., 38, 74, 176
Life after death, 63–67, 90–91,
150–51
Light of Christ, 132–34
Lineage, 114–18, 123–24
Lucifer. *See* Satan
Luther, Martin, 165

Sin: original, 33; overcoming,
33–35; Christ atoned for, 48–
52; cleansed by Holy Ghost,
82; remitted by partaking of
sacrament, 86; absence of,
during Millennium, 160–61
Smith, Hyrum, 11
Smith, Joseph, Jr.: birth of, 5;
first vision of, 6–9; receives
priesthood, 9–10, 98, 101;
organizes Church, 10–11; mar-
tyrdom of, 11; translates Book
of Mormon, 20–23; and Doctrine and Covenants, 23–24;
and Pearl of Great Price, 24;
translates Bible, 25–26; as dispensation head, 45, 165; and
concept of Zion, 105; ancient
prophets appear to, 114; as
descendant of Abraham, 123;
receives keys to gather Israel,
124; ability of, to communicate spiritual things, 127–28;
introduces Word of Wisdom,
147; restoration through, 163;
Latter-day Saints do not worship, 164; leadership of
Church after death of, 167;
and polygamy, 172
—Teachings of: on Bible, 14, 17;
on revelation, 15–16, 100–101,
129, 130; on scriptures, 27; on
Godhead, 28; on God as
exalted man, 29–30, 169; on
Holy Ghost, 32, 83; on Adam's
transgression, 32; on truth, 36;
on God's knowledge, 38; on
angels, 39; on Christ as Savior,
46, 53; on gospel preached to
all dispensations, 46–47; on
war in heaven, 58; on physical
body, 60; on suffering, 61; on
death, 64; on man as own tor-

menter, 65; on kingdoms of
glory, 66–67, 176; on ordinances, 80; on baptism, 81–82;
on being born again, 84; on
eternal marriage, 89; on work
for dead, 90, 91, 98; on Church
organization, 94; on need for a
church, 95; on gaining knowledge, 95; on First Presidency,
101; on kingdom of God, 104;
on music, 107; on Zion, 109,
112; on foreordination, 115;
on temple, 122; on spirituality, 126; on prayer, 128–29; on
learning from God, 131–32; on
false spirits, 135; on receiving
eternal life, 136; on progress-
ing toward perfection, 138; on
Millennium, 160; on Book of
Mormon, 170; on government
of heaven, 173; on blacks and
priesthood, 177
Smith, Joseph, Sr., 5
Smith, Joseph, III, 167
Smith, Joseph F., 23–24, 47–48
Smith, Joseph Fielding, 157, 169
Smith, Lucy Mack, 5
Smith, Silas, 15
Snow, Erastus, 111
Social Services, 147
Sons of perdition, 67–68, 161–62
Spirit: unembodied, 39–40; dis-
embodied, 40; children of
God, 56–57, 128, 203–4, 211;
world, 64–65, 90–91; prison,
65, 91; growth of, in premortal
world, 115
Spirituality, 126–29
Stakes of Zion, 109–10, 111
Standard works, 19. See also
Scripture
Stark, Rodney, 149
Stewardship, 105–6

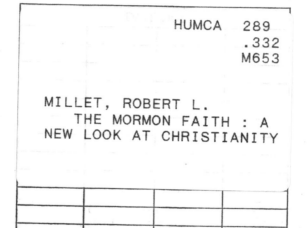